TAKE CONTROL OF OCD

TAKE CONTROL OF OCD

The Ultimate Guide for Kids With OCD

Bonnie Zucker, Psy.D.

PRUFROCK PRESS INC.
WACO, TEXAS

Library of Congress Cataloging-in-Publication Data

Zucker, Bonnie, 1974-
Take control of OCD : the ultimate guide for kids with OCD / Bonnie Zucker.
     p. cm.
 Includes bibliographical references.
 ISBN 978-1-59363-429-2 (pbk.)
1. Obsessive-compulsive disorder in children. I. Title.
 RJ506.O25Z83 2010
 618.92'85227--dc22
                              2010034863

Edited by Lacy Compton

Cover Design by Marjorie Parker

Layout Design by Raquel Trevino

ISBN-13: 978-1-59363-429-2

Printed in the United States of America.

At the time of this book's publication, all facts and figures cited are the most current available. All telephone
numbers, addresses, and Web site URLs are accurate and active. All publications, organizations, websites, and
other resources exist as described in the book, and all have been verified. The author and Prufrock Press Inc.
make no warranty or guarantee concerning the information and materials given out by organizations or content
found at websites, and we are not responsible for any changes that occur after this book's publication. If you find
an error, please contact Prufrock Press Inc.

Prufrock Press Inc.
P.O. Box 8813
Waco, TX 76714-8813
Phone: (800) 998-2208
Fax: (800) 240-0333
http://www.prufrock.com

DEDICATION

For Isaac

Your sweetness
Your light
Your happy laughter
Bring me the purest and greatest joy
I have ever known.

ACKNOWLEDGEMENTS

It is my privilege to be a therapist to so many extraordinary children and adults, who have opened their worlds to me, sharing their struggles and trusting me to guide them well. Week after week, their dedication to their psychological well-being and perseverance in facing their fear, shows their inner strength and truest resilience. Their growth and progress are my greatest achievements.

I have had the good fortune to have truly excellent teachers in many forms, teachers who have not only contributed to my knowledge, but also inspired an inner awareness that has been key to my success. Dr. Rudy Bauer has been of profound influence in my life and has offered more to me than he could ever know (although he probably knows!). Liz Marx has sparked tremendous growth in both my body and my mind. Drs. Bernard Vittone and Mary Alvord, whose unwavering confidence in me has been a treasured gift, have influenced me as a clinician in immeasurable ways. In addition, Dr. Vittone's assistance on the medication portion of this book was a tremendous help! Finally, I would not be a psychologist if it weren't for Dr. Harvey Parker's kind heart and meaningful presence in my life.

Thank you to Dr. Judith Rapoport, who so generously agreed to review this book! Her contributions to the treatment of childhood obsessive-compulsive disorder are monumental. A special thank you to Dr. Adrian Wells for his willingness to review the portions of the book on metacognitive therapy.

Lacy Compton's editorial excellence and outstanding guidance have been invaluable in the process of writing this book.

My family and friends have been a constant source of support. Paramount among them is my husband, Brian. His support of my professional growth (and often overcommitted professional life) has not only been necessary, but has also highlighted his respect for me and the passion I have for my work. And perhaps most importantly, he reminds me of the importance of getting out of my head and watching a little reality TV!

My mother has always been there for me, unconditionally, providing much love and unfailing support. Her early teachings of compassion and the importance of having direction and determination have shaped my path in life. Ilene and Norm have provided great encouragement, always cheering me on and celebrating my achievements. I thank Lisa for her constant support and genuine enthusiasm for all that I do. Emily's best friendship and sisterhood are cherished gifts; I thank her for her wisdom and her love.

CONTENTS

A NOTE FOR YOUR PARENTS

(Have your parents read this page!)

Congratulations on having your child read this book! Witnessing your child's struggle with OCD can be heart-breaking, frustrating, and anxiety-provoking for you. In addition, failed attempts at helping your child cope with this problem likely leave you with a deep sense of hopelessness.

It is a huge challenge to watch your child suffer from this anxiety disorder (and many families deal with it for years before getting help); perhaps even more challenging are the constant accommodations that you make to try to help him feel more secure and comfortable. Warm, loving, well-intentioned parents find themselves bending over backwards to help their child avoid OCD-inducing situations; yet these attempts end up reinforcing the OCD, making it stronger.

Well, there is hope! This book is your hope! Based on empirically supported treatment strategies, this book uses the cognitive-behavioral approach to guide your child through the process of taking control of OCD. Step by step, your child will learn how to understand her OCD, identify its triggers, develop a hierarchy (ladder) to use in facing her fears, learn relaxation and stress management strategies, and discover how to challenge obsessive thoughts and repetitive worries. Most importantly, your child will learn to gradually face her fears and prevent herself from engaging in rituals/compulsions that were used to reduce the anxiety stemming from the obsessive thoughts or images. She will learn how to cope with anxiety, practice mindfulness, tolerate uncertainty, and push herself to stay outside of her comfort zone.

Throughout the process, your child is encouraged to request and receive support from you and possibly others he trusts. The best advice I have is to meet your child where he is, respect his process for working through this program, and support him in any effort he makes. You may be asked to participate in the "exposure" phase when he faces his fears and exposes himself to a previously avoided situation. Offering your presence, help with making the exposures happen, and on-the-spot encouragement will be valuable gifts for your child. Finally, make sure to congratulate your child and celebrate his or her progress along the way!

Best wishes,
Dr. Bonnie Zucker

INTRODUCTION
How to Use This Book

Let me start by congratulating you for picking up this book; by starting this book today, you are making a very smart decision—to **take control of OCD**! If you suffer from Obsessive-Compulsive Disorder (OCD), you know the hold it has had on your life, how it has influenced you, and surely, at times, how it has made things very difficult for you. Reading this book is a huge step in the direction of stopping the OCD from running your life, and by using the strategies here, you will gain the freedom you want and deserve!

To be clear, the fact that you have been suffering all of this time does not mean that you haven't tried to stop the OCD; in fact, trying but not being able to get rid of the OCD is part of having the disorder. And it's not your fault that you have it. Having OCD doesn't mean that you are bad, or that you aren't normal, and it doesn't mean that you can't live a great life. It has nothing to do with how capable you are, how successful you are or will be, or how smart you are (in fact, most people with OCD are extremely bright). It only means that you have OCD, which is a type of anxiety disorder.

By deciding to start this book and follow the program described in it, you are starting the process of feeling better. The book is divided into 10 chapters, and you should read them in order and do the work that is involved. For example, Chapter 3 is called Developing Your Ladder and asks that you make a list of all of the things that are hard for you to do because of OCD; making this ladder (and actually writing all of the things on the steps of the ladder) is a necessary part of challenging the OCD. Making an actual ladder (on paper or poster board) will drastically improve your chances of having success in overcoming the OCD. So, reading the chapters and doing the work is key! It might feel like a lot of work to do, but keep in mind that the OCD itself takes a lot of work—it is time-consuming and interferes with your life. It's better to do the work in this book than to do the work that OCD requires.

The first chapter describes OCD and lists common obsessions and compulsions; Chapter 2 explains how to overcome OCD, as mentioned; Chapter 3 is about making your ladder; Chapter 4 teaches you relaxation strategies; Chapter 5 is about challenging the thoughts and worries related to the OCD; Chapter 6 explains how to deal with uncertainty; Chapters 7 and 8 teach you how to face your fears though "exposure"; Chapter 9 discusses how to manage stress; and finally, Chapter 10 is a celebration of your hard work and gives you ideas about how to deal with OCD symptoms if they come up again.

Many readers will find it helpful to ask their parents for help when using this book, while others will want to keep it to themselves. Either way will work, and it's just a matter of what feels right to you.

Throughout the book, I will describe examples of kids with OCD. These are descriptions of children I have worked with over the years, but their names and identifying information have been changed to protect their privacy.

Even though I haven't met you in person, I want you to know that I am extremely proud of you for reading this book and for doing the work you are about to do. It won't always be super easy, but if you stick with it (even through the sticky parts), you will come out on top! You will feel better, and **you will take control of OCD**!

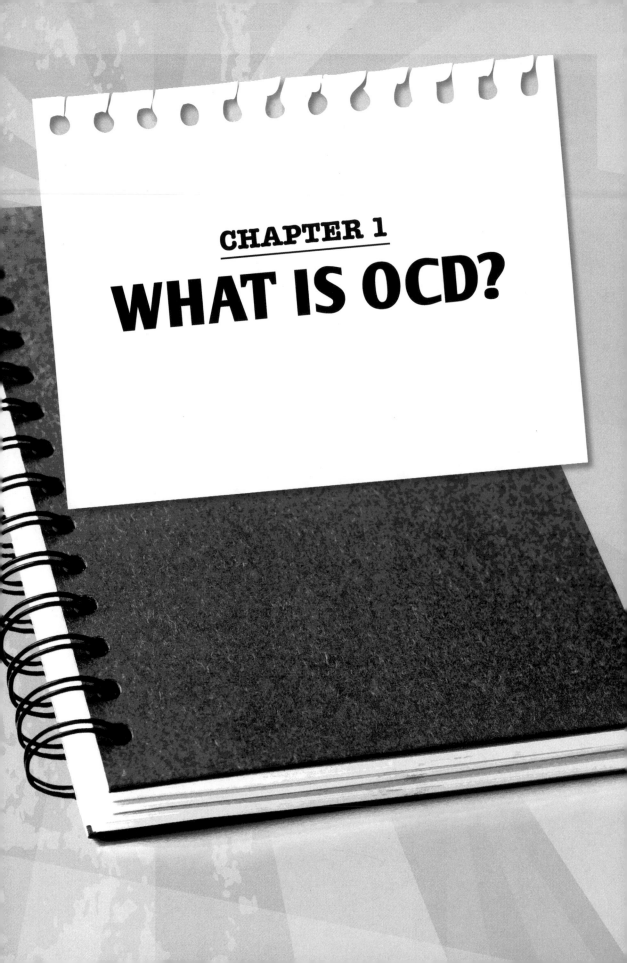

CHAPTER 1
WHAT IS OCD?

"I never really liked things like sharing drinks or using bathrooms in the mall. But about a year ago, it really became a problem for me. I couldn't stop thinking about being contaminated and all the things I touched and who I was near. At first, the rituals were small and not a big deal—I would just wash one more time, or ask one little question to check if someone was not sick. Over time, however, they became more detailed and involved, and took much longer. Eventually, it felt like most of my time was spent either thinking about these fears or doing something to try to make them better, like washing again and again and moving seats if someone at the table had been sick."

—Andrew, age 12

OCD stands for Obsessive-Compulsive Disorder, which is a type of anxiety disorder. Anxiety is a state of feeling nervous and/or being scared, and anxiety disorders are the most common psychological problem in children and adults. Obsessive-Compulsive Disorder is characterized by having the same thought or idea over and over, which usually is followed by doing some repetitive behavior.

OCD involves obsessions and/or compulsions. To have OCD, you have to have either obsessions or compulsions, but most people have both. Obsessions are thoughts, ideas, images, or urges, while compulsions are behaviors, rituals, or mental actions (things you do in your mind like counting) that usually are done to make the obsessions bet-ter. Obsessions are repetitive, meaning that they occur over and over, and they cause a feeling of anxiety or distress. Compulsions also tend to be repetitive, and the person does the behavior or ritual over and over, usually to try to feel better about the

obsessions: thoughts, ideas, images, or urges

compulsions: behaviors, rituals, or mental actions

obsessions. For example, a classic type of OCD is "contamination" type, where you may touch a bathroom door handle and begin to think obsessively about germs or being infected with an illness (this is the "obsession"). These thoughts occur again and again and cause you to feel very worried and uncomfortable. Then, as a way of dealing with the repetitive and disturbing thoughts about germs (and resulting anxiety), you wash you hands several times. Washing your hands is the "compulsive" behavior, or ritual, that you do to try to get rid of the germs (and the thoughts about the germs). Usually the washing is excessive, meaning that you will wash for a long time and will rewash and rewash your hands. The problem is that the hand-washing becomes a repetitive behavior (something you do again and again) and only works to get rid of the obsessive thoughts for the short term. In the long term, the OCD is becoming stronger.

A symptom is a sign that something is wrong; for instance, sneezing and coughing are symptoms of a cold. Similarly, obsessions and compulsions are symptoms of OCD. To be "diagnosed" with OCD, the obsessions and compulsions need to make you feel distressed (very upset), need to take more than 1 hour a day, and need to interfere with your normal activities like school, social activities, or relationships with others. Because the symptoms of OCD are distracting, it can be hard to concentrate on things like schoolwork. Because the symptoms of OCD are time-consuming, it can be hard to spend time with friends and family in a normal way and be on time to places like school and social events.

To be "diagnosed" with OCD, the obsessions and compulsions:

> ➤ need to make the person feel distressed (very upset),

> ➤ need to take more than 1 hour a day, and

> ➤ need to interfere with normal activities like school, social activities, or relationships with others.

Obsessions are not just regular worries about real-life situations like having a project due for school or having an argument with a friend. Instead, obsessions are usually about unrealistic or impossible threats (e.g., getting cancer from bathrooms, being punished by God). About 1 in 200 children and teens have OCD; there is a strong relationship between childhood and adulthood OCD, meaning that if it isn't addressed and treated when you're young, it will likely continue when you're an adult.

Although each person with OCD will experience different symptoms, there are some common themes and types of obsessions and compulsions:

Types of Obsessions

- ➤ Contamination (thinking about being infected with germs)
- ➤ Repeated doubts (wondering if you did or didn't do something like leave a door unlocked)
- ➤ Desire for certainty (needing to know for sure that you did or didn't do something)
- ➤ Symmetry (needing things to be in a certain order or doing things in a way that "just feels right")
- ➤ Scrupulosity (having religious/moral doubt; experiencing disturbing sexual thoughts or urges)
- ➤ Indecisiveness (not being able to decide until it "feels right")
- ➤ "Just feels right" (getting stuck on something because it doesn't "feel right" to you such as feeling like the way you touched the table wasn't the "right" way or feeling like the word you said wasn't the "right" word to use)

Types of Compulsions

- ➤ Washing/cleaning
- ➤ Checking
- ➤ Needing to ask/tell/ confess
- ➤ Counting
- ➤ Ordering/arranging
- ➤ Repeating actions
- ➤ Waiting until it "feels right"
- ➤ Praying
- ➤ Asking for reassurance (e.g., asking others to tell you it will be OK)
- ➤ Hoarding (saving a great amount of stuff and refusing to get rid of any of it)

Children and teens with OCD usually feel driven to do the compulsive behaviors and feel that they cannot control the urge to do the behaviors. Compulsions are usually done to lessen the distress caused by the obsession. Compulsions also can be done because the person thinks that doing them will prevent something bad from happening (for example, walking in a certain way to protect someone you love). Sometimes, compulsions involve rigid or stereotyped actions that are completed according to self-created, very detailed rules (for example, ordering your books from shortest to tallest in a very specific order while saying the alphabet). Most people have a hard time explaining *why* they are doing the compulsions. They often know that the compulsions don't make sense, but the urge to do them is very, very strong.

OCD CYCLE

There is a pattern to how OCD gets triggered (meaning how it gets "set off"). Although sometimes it simply comes up (e.g., an idea just pops into your head and you get stuck on the thought), there often is an order to how the OCD plays out:

1. Event (trigger situation)
2. Thought (obsession/obsessive thought or image)
3. Feeling (anxiety, fear, discomfort)
4. Action (compulsion/compulsive behavior)

Dr. Bruce Hyman and Cherry Pedrick (2005) explained it in a similar way:

1. "Activating Event"
2. "Unrealistic Appraisal of Event"
3. "Excessive Anxiety"
4. "Neutralizing Ritual"

To make the OCD cycle clear, let's go through a few examples. Here are examples, going from simple to more complicated and involved.

OCD CYCLE

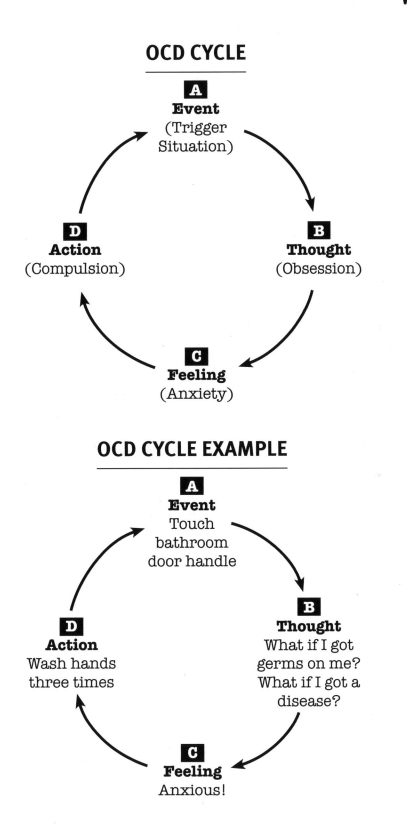

A
Event
(Trigger
Situation)

B
Thought
(Obsession)

C
Feeling
(Anxiety)

D
Action
(Compulsion)

OCD CYCLE EXAMPLE

A
Event
Touch
bathroom
door handle

B
Thought
What if I got
germs on me?
What if I got a
disease?

C
Feeling
Anxious!

D
Action
Wash hands
three times

Example 1:
Andrew, 12 years old,
OCD: Contamination Type

Event: Use public bathroom

Thought: I can't touch the toilet, flusher, faucets, or doorknob because there are dangerous germs on all of them. Maybe I touched someone's germs and will get sick.

Feeling: Very, very anxious!

Action: Wash hands and use paper towels to turn off faucet and open doorknob.

Example 2:
Alicia, 11 years old,
OCD: Contamination Type

Event: Eat cookie from bake sale

Thought: What if the person who baked it was sick? Now I will get their germs and be sick, too! The eggs could have salmonella in them, or the ingredients could be old and expired! What if I throw up?

Feeling: Very, very anxious!

Action: Ask Mom for reassurance that the cookies were safe. Ask friends if they ate cookies from the bake sale and see how they are feeling. Wait 3 days until I feel sure that I didn't get sick from bake sale cookies.

Example 3:
Sydney, 10 years old, OCD:
Doubting/Indecisiveness Types

Event: Step on something

Thought: What if I stepped on a bug and killed it?

Feeling: Very, very anxious!

Action: Go back and check sidewalk.

Example 4:
Jasmine, 15 years old, OCD:
Symmetry/"Just Feels Right" Types

Event: Look at desk

Thought: Things are out of order. They need to be straight.

Feeling: Very, very uncomfortable!

Action: Order and arrange everything until it is all lined up.

Example 5:
William, 16 years old,
OCD: Scrupulosity Type

Event: Asked to go to a party with friends

Thought: I shouldn't have fun or else I will be punished. Something bad will happen if I enjoy myself and feel pleasure.

Feeling: Very, very anxious!

Action: Tell my friends that I can't go. Stay home and do homework instead.

> **Example 6:**
> Kevin, 14 years old,
> OCD: Scrupulosity Type
>
> **Event:** Walk by a park with other kids playing
>
> **Thought:** What if I hurt one of those kids or touched their privates? What if someone knew my thoughts? Does thinking it mean that I did it? Is it as bad as doing it?
>
> **Feeling:** Very, very anxious!
>
> **Action:** Shake head four times to the right, quickly and forcefully.

In Chapter 3, we will go through these examples in more detail, and you will see the ladders that each of these children used to face their OCD.

There also are children who have OCD that doesn't follow the cycle described above. For example, there often can be an obsessive image that is not a thought. Eleven-year-old Mark would see lines all over the place when he walked into rooms. His mind just "saw" these connecting lines, and it was very hard for him to concentrate and think clearly because the lines he saw all over the place made it difficult for him to notice other things. Fifteen-year-old Ashley would get stuck on certain mathematical formulas, such as seeing two perpendicular lines, and would obsessively think about the point at which they connected/intersected and how that point was "double counted" in that it was part of two different lines. For both Mark and Ashley, their compulsions made them focus on and think about the lines and math formulas until they reached a point when it "felt right" or "felt OK," and then they could focus on something else.

CAUSES OF OCD

It is not completely clear what causes OCD, but it is clear that it involves certain parts of the brain working differently than they should. Although there is nothing wrong with the *structure* of the brain, there is miscommunication between some of the different parts. As a result, the brain sort of hiccups, and you end up getting stuck on the same thought—which is the OCD.

Most researchers believe OCD is something you are born with (meaning that it is genetic), and it simply comes out at a certain point as you are growing up. Because OCD symptoms worsen with stress, it also is important to consider that children who are born with the tendency to have OCD may have it come out during or after a period of high stress. Parents cannot cause OCD in their children out of the blue; however, if their child has the genes for OCD in the first place, parents may do things that cause the OCD to come out. For example, it is possible that a child's parent has OCD and models OCD behaviors that the child ends up learning to do as well. This is called "modeling," and when this happens, it is not because the parent meant to teach their child OCD behaviors. Also, parents who are very demanding and perfectionistic or overly critical with their children may increase the chances that their children will develop OCD; but again, this is not done on purpose.

There is current research that suggests that a small number of children may develop OCD (or their OCD may worsen) after having a certain form of strep throat. In these cases, the OCD symptoms come up suddenly and intensely. These rare cases of OCD are called PANDAS (Pediatric Autoimmune Neuropsychiatric Disorder Associated with Strep) and require typical OCD treatment (see Chapter 2) plus antibiotics to cure the infection. There is still more research needed on this topic.

Most of your characteristics—the color of your eyes, if math comes naturally or not, if you have allergies—are determined by your genes. You are born a certain way, and this cannot be changed; nor would you want to change it, because you are unique and were born with great characteristics. We don't want to change *you*! However, OCD is just like if you have allergies— you treat them by seeing a doctor and perhaps taking allergy medication, you make sure that your house is clean and not dusty, and you clear out your nose with steam or a Neti pot. By doing these things, you end up not suffering from allergies. Similarly, by learning how to treat OCD, you will end up not suffering from it anymore.

This is the *good news*: OCD is very treatable, meaning that you can work through this program and overcome the disorder. Also, there is research that shows you can change how your brain works by training your brain to respond a different way. It is your decision to overcome OCD and it will be your hard work that will make this a success! It won't always be easy, but it will work—you can do it!

OTHER COMMON PROBLEMS

It is very common for children with OCD to have another anxiety disorder and/or a mood disorder such as depression. About 50%–70% of children and teens with OCD also will have another psychological disorder, most commonly another anxiety disorder, ADHD, or a mood disorder. The goal is to treat the other disorder in addition to treating the OCD. Usually when the OCD improves, the other anxiety or mood disorder will improve as well. It is important to know that the other disorder does impact the treatment process and might need to be addressed as well. The other disorder also may influence the kind of medications you may take (explained in the next chapter); for example, stimulant medication prescribed for ADHD has been shown to make OCD symptoms worse.

Other anxiety disorders include:
➤ *generalized anxiety*: constantly worrying, usually about a lot of different things, accompanied by feeling restless, having muscle tension, and finding it hard to concentrate;
➤ *separation anxiety*: having a very hard time separating from your mom or dad, or the main caregiver, and often not wanting to be alone or sleep alone at night;
➤ *social anxiety*: worrying about being judged negatively by others, which makes it hard to join new groups, express your preferences, raise your hand in class, and perform in front of others;

➤ *panic attacks*: having a very strong feeling of fear that causes a lot of physical anxiety, including rapid heartbeat or heart palpitations, difficulty breathing or feelings of choking, dizziness/lightheadedness, trembling/shaking, tingling or numbness in your hands or feet, fear of dying, fear of going crazy, feeling like you are not in your body; panic attacks come on and peak, then start to decrease; and

➤ *specific phobia*: being very scared of something, such as dogs, flying on an airplane, or getting a shot; you either avoid the thing you are terrified of, or you get extremely distressed while near it.

Sometimes, the OCD comes on first, and when it doesn't go away or get treated, you end up becoming depressed. Sometimes depression comes first and then OCD appears later. Depression is when you feel sad for most days of the week and find it hard to break away from the sadness or to feel better. Depression makes you feel less interested in activities that you used to enjoy. Children with depression may cry or tear up easily, feel bad about themselves or feel guilty, feel tired or have low energy, have trouble sleeping or sleep too much, not eat enough or overeat, and especially in boys, be very irritable or agitated. Usually, children with depression just feel this way, maybe out of the blue, rather than having an event cause them to be depressed. When there is an event that happens that causes a child to feel very sad or depressed, such as when a best friend moves away or when parents get divorced, this is *not* called a depressive disorder. Instead, it is a normal reaction to an upsetting event. Depression can be serious and can sometimes make children think about death or about killing themselves. If this happens to you, you should talk

comorbidity: when you have two disorders at the same time; if you have OCD and another anxiety disorder, that second anxiety disorder is called a comorbid disorder

to your parents, or to another caring adult, and get professional help immediately. With treatment, depression will improve.

Now that you know what OCD is, let's move on to discussing how we can treat it.

What I Know Now

In this chapter, you learned the definition of OCD and the common types of obsessions and compulsions. We reviewed the OCD cycle: (1) triggering event, (2) thought (obsession), (3) feeling (anxiety), and (4) action (compulsion, ritual), and we went through several examples to better understand how the cycle works. Then you learned about the causes of OCD and how we can change how the brain works! Finally, you learned about other common co-occurring problems, that OCD is a treatable disorder, and that by following this program, you can overcome it!

CHAPTER 2
HOW TO OVERCOME OCD

"OCD had taken a huge toll on my life and prevented me from living fully and completely. However, I found out that there are steps you can take to reduce your anxious symptoms and more fully enjoy life."

—William, age 16

Starting right now, I would like you to think differently about OCD. Instead of it being a part of you, I'd like you to begin thinking about it as something separate. It is YOU versus OCD. This is called "externalizing the OCD." Because you've had OCD symptoms, they have likely felt like they were a part of you. But now you need to start thinking of OCD as separate, as something you can challenge directly, just like if you were playing against someone in a sport or a game. You want to think about that other player and the moves he or she is going to make to learn how to have a good offense and defense. The more you understand how OCD works—how it tries to gain power over you, what it says to you, how it gets stronger in certain situations—the easier it will be to win against it!

The first step is to understand your symptoms and how OCD impacts your life—what behaviors you do and don't do in response to OCD, and what situations you avoid because of OCD. In the upcoming chapters, you will list the situations that you avoid, and this will set the stage for overcoming OCD. You also will learn how to identify when OCD is "talking to you" by making a list called "When my OCD talks, it says . . ."—this list will help you understand when OCD is trying to influence you. You will learn many strategies and techniques to overcome OCD and minimize its impact on your life. You will learn ways not to be "organized" by OCD, meaning that OCD won't influence how you do things and live your life.

externalizing the OCD: when you think about OCD as something separate, instead of it being a part of you; it's you vs. OCD

COGNITIVE-BEHAVIORAL THERAPY

The research on OCD shows that the best approach to treating it is cognitive-behavioral therapy (CBT). Other types of therapy have not been proven to work for children with OCD.

CBT explains that OCD (like all anxiety disorders) has three parts:

1. body
2. thoughts
3. behavior

When you are anxious and having OCD symptoms, it comes out in your body, thoughts, and behavior. Your **body** feels different when you are completely relaxed than it does when you are stressed out, worried, or scared. Obsessive thoughts and ideas and worries are the **thoughts** part: you will worry, have certain thinking patterns, and think certain thoughts to yourself when you are focused on obsessions. Your actions or **behavior** will be different when you are stuck in the OCD cycle compared to when you are not.

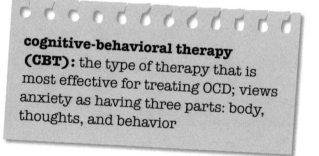

cognitive-behavioral therapy (CBT): the type of therapy that is most effective for treating OCD; views anxiety as having three parts: body, thoughts, and behavior

Below is a list of common body, thought, and behavioral symptoms related to OCD:

Common Body Symptoms
➤ Muscle tension
➤ Fast heartbeat
➤ Sweaty palms
➤ Shallow breathing
➤ Stomachaches
➤ Feeling dizzy or lightheaded
➤ Hot flushes

Common Thought Symptoms
➤ Worries
➤ Obsessive thoughts or ideas
➤ Thinking errors/mistakes
➤ Negative self-talk
➤ Doubting, questioning

Common Behavioral Symptoms
➤ Compulsions/rituals (washing, checking, ordering, repeating, confessing)
➤ Avoidance of situations
➤ Nervous behaviors

Below is a diagram of the three parts, including descriptions of each part:

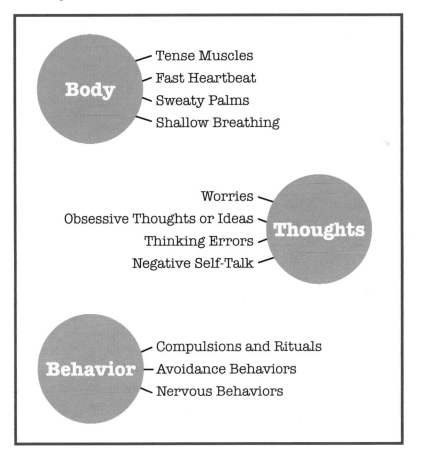

To treat OCD, we need to address all three parts: body, thoughts, and behavior. Chapter 4 is about relaxation, which deals with the body; Chapters 5 and 6 address the thoughts part; and Chapters 7 and 8 focus on changing your behavior. You will learn how to calm and relax your body, identify and challenge obsessive thinking patterns, replace worried thoughts with realistic ones, master worries, talk back to OCD with positive self-talk, and experience your thoughts differently by learning mindfulness and similar techniques. You also will learn how to be comfortable with not having certainty, or not knowing

> **exposure:** when you purposely practice being in an anxiety or trigger situation, as a way of facing your fears

for sure, you will be able to do this by learning "uncertainty training." To stop doing the compulsions, you will learn how to face your fears. Once you know the strategies, you will be ready to "expose" yourself to the OCD situations and stop engaging in rituals and other compulsions. You will do this with exposure/response prevention.

EXPOSURE/RESPONSE PREVENTION (E/RP)

Exposure/response prevention (E/RP) is the best way to overcome OCD because it involves being "exposed" to the situations that you avoid because of OCD and then not doing your typical response (ritual). When you are exposed to the situations you avoid, this is called an "exposure." Doing an exposure is when you purposely practice being in an anxiety

> **exposure/response prevention (E/RP):** being "exposed" to the situations that you avoid because of OCD and then not doing your typical response (ritual)

or trigger situation (one which triggers your OCD) as a way of facing your fears. For example, if you worry about being contaminated by germs and wash your hands repeatedly to feel better about this worry, then you would purposely "contaminate" yourself by touching a doorknob and then not washing your hands.

To make this process easier, you will take small steps to get to this point. For example, you may start by touching the doorknob, waiting 3 minutes, and then washing your hands; then, you will build up tolerance by doing this repeatedly, until you get to the point of opening and closing doors entirely without washing your hands! You will do this with all of your avoided or feared situations—so that you will be left with no obsessive rituals. Now, this is the point where you might consider putting this book down or throwing it, begin thinking that this Dr. Zucker is crazy, or simply stop reading! But DON'T do any of that! You should stay with this book and follow this program for three reasons:

1. You don't want OCD to rule your life anymore and take away the freedom you want and deserve.
2. You will learn many techniques to deal with the anxiety that comes from not doing the rituals, so it won't be *as* hard as you imagine. Plus, you are in charge of your program—YOU will decide the pace and number of steps you want to break it into.
3. Dr. Zucker is not crazy and she has used this program with hundreds of kids just like you and all of these children have overcome their OCD and anxiety! They are no longer ruled by OCD. You are NO different from all of these other kids—you can do it too!

Remember that before we start E/RP, you will learn many ways to manage the anxiety and uncomfortable feelings that come up when you prevent yourself from doing the compulsive behaviors and rituals. It won't always be easy, but you are 100% capable of doing this. This is how you will be a master at challenging OCD; this is how you will win!

METACOGNITIVE THERAPY (MCT)

A psychologist named Dr. Adrian Wells, from the United Kingdom, developed a type of cognitive therapy called "metacognitive therapy" (MCT). MCT focuses on your relationship to your thoughts and *how* you think (instead of *what* you think). Metacognition is a basic inner process that is in charge of managing your thinking. Metacognition is responsible for shaping what you focus on and pay attention to. Dr. Wells explained that people with anxiety disorders like OCD get their attention stuck on threatening things. He called this problem "cognitive attentional syndrome," which is made up of worry, repetitive thinking patterns, and the tendency to scan the environment for threats.

metacognitive therapy (MCT): a type of cognitive therapy that focuses on your relationship to your thoughts and how you think (instead of what you think)

MCT tries to help people understand their beliefs about their thoughts. For example, you might believe that by thinking about all of the ways that germs can get to you, you are then able to prevent getting contaminated or getting sick. This is a belief that you have formed about your thoughts.

The goal of metacognitive therapy is to change the way you experience and relate to your thoughts and to change how you react to your thoughts or ideas. There are two main MCT techniques that help you switch your attention away from its focus on threat and change the way you experience your thoughts: the attention training technique and the detached mindfulness technique.

1. Attention Training Technique

This technique helps you learn how to switch your focus from one thing to another and how to divide your attention between more than one thing at once.

For more information on this technique, I recommend that you have your parent(s) or a professional therapist refer to Dr. Wells's book (see the references section in the back of this book) and look at Chapter 4, which gives a script for the technique. Your parent or therapist can do the recording of the script for you, and you can listen to it twice a day until you are able to master switching your focus and attention away from the OCD-related thoughts. You should listen to the script when you are not anxious or stressed.

2. Detached Mindfulness Technique

This technique teaches you how to be aware (or mindful) of your thoughts and how to become an observer of your thoughts (detachment), rather than a responder to your thoughts. In detached mindfulness, you learn how to recognize that your thought is just a thought. Whether it is true or not, it is only a thought, and nothing else. This will help you to be less reactive to what you are actually thinking about, because you will learn how to see the thought as just a thought.

Because this is a different way of thinking about your thoughts, it may sound a little confusing to you. I admit, when I first learned about metacognitive therapy, it took a while for me to really understand the technique and what it had to say about the thoughts part of OCD.

By learning about MCT, you can gain another strategy to use to overcome OCD, as it teaches you how to change your beliefs about your thoughts and how to shift your focus away from OCD-related thoughts.

MINDFULNESS

Just as detached mindfulness in MCT teaches you a different way of seeing your thoughts, traditional mindfulness describes a different way of experiencing yourself and the world—almost like a different way of seeing things. During most of your day-to-day life, you are thinking about and focused on what you are doing; whether it's homework, talking to friends, or watching TV, you likely go through your days busy with thoughts. Having OCD, you also likely worry and get upset about OCD-related thoughts and situations. Worries are thoughts about things that haven't happened yet; in fact, they often are about things that will probably never happen (even though it doesn't feel that way at the time). Worries are about the future, and because they are about the future, they distract you from focusing on what is happening right now, in the present moment.

One goal in dealing with anxiety and OCD is to help you be more focused on

mindfulness: the process of being fully aware of yourself and your thoughts

being in the present moment, and mindfulness helps you learn how to do this. Like detached mindfulness described above, mindfulness allows you to gain distance from your thoughts (by identifying them as thoughts) and simply be in the moment. When you are focused on this exact moment, you will realize that you are OK.

Mindfulness is the process of being fully aware of yourself and your thoughts. When OCD symptoms come up, your focus gets narrow and you are drawn into the obsessions and compulsions. This can be an automatic process. To prevent this from happening, and to make it possible to change the OCD pattern, you want to take a step back and be aware that you are stuck in OCD thinking. You want to refocus on the present moment, rather than staying stuck on an OCD thought.

Through learning mindfulness, you will learn that OCD is just a thought. When someone has OCD, they get into the habit of regularly having OCD thoughts. Mindfulness is a way to get away from your thoughts in a very pleasant and relaxed way. The deeper part of mindfulness is that it helps you get out of your mind—not in a scary way, or in a way that makes you feel not like yourself, but in an incredibly peaceful way that not only makes you feel like you are OK, but also actually shows you that you are.

It helps you be less focused on your thoughts, and more focused on the actual experience at hand.

Though practicing mindfulness and learning how to meditate (Chapter 4), you will experience what it feels like to be less attached to your thoughts. This will make it easier to challenge the OCD, as it will be easier to see the OCD as a thought that you can either focus on or not (like in detached mindfulness described above).

Now that we have reviewed the different approaches to overcoming OCD in detail, let's look at the three parts again, this time with added descriptions of the approaches. The arrows point to the methods you will use to address each part.

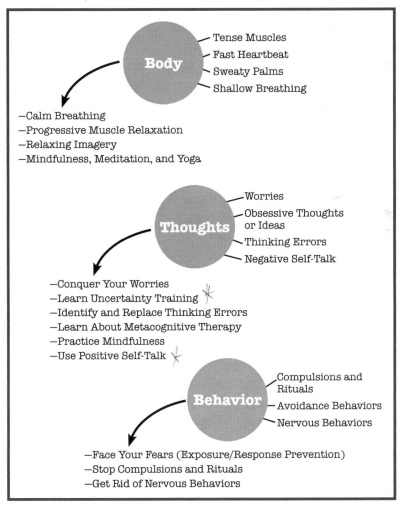

Body
- Tense Muscles
- Fast Heartbeat
- Sweaty Palms
- Shallow Breathing

—Calm Breathing
—Progressive Muscle Relaxation
—Relaxing Imagery
—Mindfulness, Meditation, and Yoga

Thoughts
- Worries
- Obsessive Thoughts or Ideas
- Thinking Errors
- Negative Self-Talk

—Conquer Your Worries
—Learn Uncertainty Training
—Identify and Replace Thinking Errors
—Learn About Metacognitive Therapy
—Practice Mindfulness
—Use Positive Self-Talk

Behavior
- Compulsions and Rituals
- Avoidance Behaviors
- Nervous Behaviors

—Face Your Fears (Exposure/Response Prevention)
—Stop Compulsions and Rituals
—Get Rid of Nervous Behaviors

MEDICATION

Many children with OCD also need medication, and this is usually prescribed by a psychiatrist. Just like there is nothing to feel bad about for having OCD, there is nothing to feel bad about for taking medication to help you treat it. Again, many people with allergies take allergy medications and get better; similarly, many kids with OCD benefit from medication.

Studies have been done to see which treatment—cognitive-behavioral therapy (CBT), medication, or both combined together—is best for children with OCD. The studies found that the combination of CBT and medication has the best results, but just doing CBT comes very close—that those kids do almost as well, on average, as the kids who have both CBT and medication. Children who *only* take medication, but don't do CBT don't do nearly as well as either of the other treatment groups. So, while CBT is most important, it may be beneficial to also take medication. However, children should not be on medication without also being in CBT.

The most common type of medication used to treat OCD is called "selective serotonin reuptake inhibitors" or SSRIs. SSRIs work in the brain to prevent the reabsorption of a neurotransmitter called "serotonin," and this ends up making more serotonin available in the brain. For some unknown reason, when there is more serotonin floating around between the neurons, OCD symptoms improve, and people have less OCD thoughts and urges. Common SSRI brand names include: Prozac, Zoloft, Luvox, and Paxil. There are also medications that are similar to SSRIs but also work on other neurotransmitters (not

selective serotonin reuptake inhibitors (SSRIs): medication that works in the brain to prevent the reabsorption of a neurotransmitter called "serotonin," making more of it available in the brain, which makes OCD improve

just serotonin); these include brand names such as Effexor and Remeron. A doctor will help you decide which medication is the best option.

Anti-anxiety medications, such as Klonopin, Xanax, and Ativan also are commonly used to help reduce the feeling of anxiety in children and teens with OCD. They often are given *in addition to* SSRIs, although they can be given alone. The main caution is that these can cause physical dependence, meaning that if you take these medications for a long period of time, you may feel like you need to keep taking them.

Finally, if the SSRIs and anti-anxiety medications are not doing the job, a low dose of mood stabilizers such as Risperdal, Zyprexa, or Seroquel could be added for additional help.

To summarize, medication should not be given unless the child also is receiving help from a therapist skilled in cognitive-behavioral therapy. Also, medication should not be the first choice, as there are side effects. Rather, therapy should be started first, and then if needed, medication should be given for additional benefit. Don't worry, though, if you are already taking medication and haven't been in therapy yet; reading this book is a great step. Finally, if you are taking medication and experience side effects, make sure to tell your parents and your doctor.

OTHER THINGS TO KEEP IN MIND

BEING PROACTIVE

To be *proactive* means to take action—to identify a problem and come up with a solution. When you are being proactive, your behavior is a result of your values—of what is important to you including your larger goals. The opposite is to be *reactive*. When you are being reactive, your behavior is a result of your feelings. Let's use the example of doing your homework. Many times, you won't feel like doing your homework. There are other things you'd rather be doing, like watching TV, playing outside, playing video games, doing your nails, reading a magazine, or just doing nothing! If you are being reactive, you won't do your homework because you will decide according to your feelings. You don't feel like it, so you won't do it. However, if you are being proactive, you will do your homework because you will decide according to your values. You don't feel like it, but that doesn't matter, because doing your homework and going to school the next day with all of your homework done—and being prepared—is important to you. In other words, it is what you value.

proactive: to take action; to identify a problem and come up with a solution based on your values (rather than your feelings)

You may not always feel like doing the work that's involved with taking control of OCD. At times, it will be hard and you will be challenged. During those times, I encourage you to be *proactive*! Keep reminding yourself that you value working through the book, you value working hard to overcome your OCD, and you value your commitment to helping yourself come out on top.

GETTING SUPPORT FROM OTHERS WHO BELIEVE IN YOU

If you were to come into my office and we were to meet in person, one of the first things I would share with you would be that I believe in you and your ability to take control of OCD. Believing in yourself and having others believe in you is very important to the success of this program. There is no reason why you cannot be 100% successful. If you put 100% in, you will get 100% out. It will start out harder and get easier as you move through it. You will learn what your own process is—what works for you, how you do best, and how you use support from others. You should respect your own process of working through this problem in your life.

Parents, siblings, other family, and close friends can offer great support, and you should pick at least one or two people who you trust and with who you feel comfortable talking about this process. Most of the children and teens I have worked with have had to involve their family members—usually their parents. This is particularly true for family members who have engaged in rituals and compulsions with you. This is very common. Loving, supportive parents end up supporting rituals sometimes, because they want you to feel better in a moment of distress. But as mentioned, the rituals and compulsions only help you in the short term, and overall they make the OCD worse. If you have parents or others who have helped you do the rituals, or who have made "accommodations" for the OCD, you will need to tell them that they will have to stop. In fact, it can be one of the steps you take in facing your fears and overcoming OCD.

Teach parents and others what you are learning in this book, and tell them how they can best support you. Would it be helpful for your mom or dad to tell you that they are proud of you or support you in other ways, like helping you practice the exposures by being there by your side? Could they help by showing affection and hugging you if you have had a tough time with the practices? The goal is to figure out how others can best help you, and to tell them or ask them directly what you want or need from them.

It is your personal choice whether to tell friends and other family members about your OCD. Although most people will be completely understanding and offer their support, some others might be judging or find it difficult to respond in a warm, appropriate way. Regardless of who you choose to tell (or not tell), or what reactions you may get from others, do not forget that OCD is a very common problem. In fact, anxiety disorders are the most common psychological issue of childhood and adulthood. There is nothing wrong with you for having OCD, and you are working hard and trying your best to take control of OCD!

Be hopeful. Don't doubt or question your strength. This can work, and it will work. Have confidence that you can and will make it work. You will do the things you need to do, step by step, and you will come out on top! You can do it!

What I Know Now

In this chapter, you learned about cognitive-behavioral therapy (CBT) and how OCD has three parts: body, thoughts, and behavior. We reviewed the common body signs, thoughts, and behaviors associated with OCD, and the methods you will learn to treat all three parts. You learned about exposure/response prevention (E/RP) and how you will break steps down into smaller steps and go at your own pace. The principles of metacognitive therapy (MCT) and mindfulness were introduced as they will be helpful, particularly for dealing with the thoughts part of OCD. The option of medication was discussed, and you learned about the common medications used to treat OCD. Finally, you learned about being proactive, being hopeful, and the importance of believing in yourself and having others believe in you.

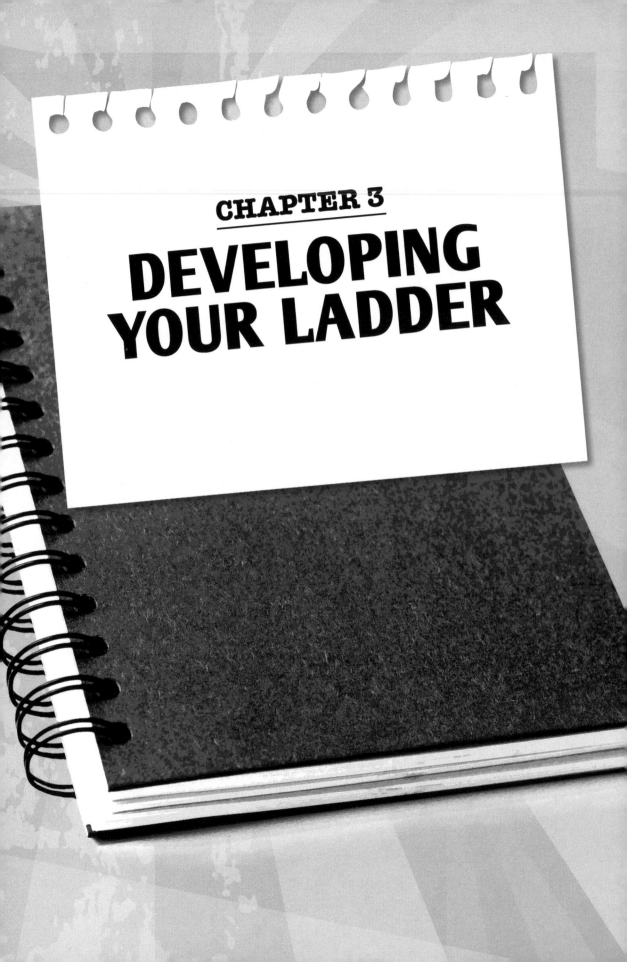

CHAPTER 3

DEVELOPING YOUR LADDER

"Listing all of the things I didn't do because of OCD made it easy to see how much of a problem it was. When we made my ladder, I thought to myself, 'I will never be able to do those steps at the top,' yet when I got to those steps, I was able to do it! All the little steps made it possible to do those at the top, plus I used many strategies that I learned to be able to deal with it."

—Olive, age 11

The purpose of this chapter is to understand how OCD impacts your life, limits what you can do, and causes you to do certain things (behaviors you do in response to OCD such as compulsions and rituals). When you are "organized" by something, you are controlled by it, and it influences what you do; when you have OCD, you end up being organized and controlled by it. Now is the time to get a clear understanding of just how much it organizes you and your behavior. With this understanding, you will begin the goal-setting part of this program.

In this chapter, you will develop your ladder. The ladder will list all of the situations that are hard for you to do because of OCD: situations that you avoid because they cause you anxiety or make you feel uncomfortable. For example, these situations might include using public bathrooms, eating food from sample trays in grocery stores, or not counting the steps when you walk up stairs.

It is important to make the ladder now—early in the book—because it sets the stage for what's to come. You will use the ladder during the exposure phase beginning in Chapter 7. Even though you will learn a lot before it comes time to do the steps on the ladder, doing it now is very helpful. It lays out the goals in the beginning of the process, and this will make it flow better later on.

MAKING YOUR LADDER

At the end of this chapter, there is a page that has a drawing of a ladder. You can choose to actually use this one and write in the book, or you can make your own ladder on a separate sheet of paper or a larger poster board. In my work with children, I cut a poster board in half and use good-smelling Mr. Sketch™ markers to make the ladder; many children choose to decorate around the margins of their posters. Whether it's decorative or not, you should try to make your ladder visually clear—so when you look at it, it's easy to read and see what steps are included.

ladder: a list of all the situations that are hard for you to do because of OCD; situations that you avoid because they cause you anxiety or make you feel uncomfortable

The first step in making your ladder is to list all of the situations that you avoid because of OCD on a separate sheet of paper. You want to write the list in a positive way, describing what you *should* or *would* be doing if you didn't have OCD. For example, if you don't touch doorknobs with your hands, you would write it as "touch doorknobs with hands"; if you do four checking ritual behaviors before you leave the house every morning, you would write it as "leave house without checking oven, toaster, back door, and Sniffy (the dog)."

If it is hard to start writing things out this way, you can first list all of the rituals and OCD behaviors that you do and all of the things you avoid. Then, you can change them over, or convert them, to describe what you should be doing, or what you would like to be able to do—like touch doorknobs with your hands.

The list should be very thorough, and you may ask your parent(s) or sibling for ideas of what to include, as they are probably aware of your OCD behaviors. Include all rituals that you do to make the obsessive thoughts, ideas, or images better; list every behavior that is done in response to the OCD thoughts.

Once you have listed all of the behaviors and rituals, and the situations that you avoid, then you want to put them in order, numbering them from easiest to stop doing to hardest. Some kids like to use note cards to write out each situation and then lay them all out on the floor and put them in order this way—laying out the easier ones on the bottom and then the harder ones on the top. You can do this, or just number the items (for example, from 1 to 15) on the sheet of paper. Every person has a different number of steps on his or her ladder. There is no set number, but I do recommend having at least 8–10 steps. Also, you can break steps down into smaller steps. Using the example above, you can break down "leave house without checking oven, toaster, back door, and Sniffy" into four steps: "leave house without checking oven," "leave house without checking oven and toaster," "leave house without checking oven, toaster, and back door," and "leave house without checking oven, toaster, back door, and Sniffy." You are in charge of deciding how many smaller steps you will break the steps down into, and this may be something that you won't decide upon until you are actually in the exposure phase (when you practice the steps).

This brings up another point: Once you are doing the exposures, you may find that you want to make changes to your ladder—either adding steps, changing the order, breaking them down further into smaller steps, or getting rid of steps that no longer fit. This may happen as your understanding of your own OCD improves. This is perfectly fine, and for this reason, it is best to leave some space in between steps on the ladder or leave a few steps blank.

To help you understand how ladders work, and maybe even get some ideas on what to include in your own ladder, let's go through the examples from Chapter 1 to show how other kids and teens made their ladders.

> **Example 1:**
> Andrew, 12 years old,
> OCD: Contamination Type
>
> **Event:** Use public bathroom
>
> **Thought:** I can't touch the toilet, flusher, faucets, or doorknob because there are dangerous germs on all of them. Maybe I touched someone's germs and will get sick.
>
> **Feeling:** Very, very anxious!
>
> **Action:** Wash hands and use paper towels to turn off faucet and open doorknob.

Andrew worried constantly about getting contaminated with germs and getting sick. He avoided any surface that he thought might have germs on it, and also avoided people who he thought might get him sick. Andrew tried his best to avoid public bathrooms, but he ended up having to use them in school. When he did use public bathrooms, he would do his best to avoid touching the lock on the door, the flusher, the sink, and the doorknob. He used paper towels and toilet paper to navigate his way through the bathroom.

List of avoided situations and OCD-related behaviors:

➤ Use public bathrooms

➤ Use public bathroom and wash hands for 15 seconds

➤ Use bathroom and wash hands for 5 seconds

➤ Use bathroom and wash hands without reciting alphabet in head

➤ Touch lock on bathroom door with hands (not sleeve)

➤ Touch toilet with hands (not toilet paper)

➤ Touch flusher with hands

➤ Touch faucet

➤ Use first paper towel from dispenser

➤ Touch doorknob or handle with hands

➤ Sit next to someone for one minute after he or she sneezed

➤ Walk by the pharmacy part of the drugstore

➤ Have lunch near a sick kid

➤ Go to a friend's house after the friend was sick last week

➤ Touch doorknobs and handles in public places

➤ Go to a friend's house without asking about recent illnesses

Once Andrew listed his items, he ranked them in order (with 1 being the easiest and 16 being the hardest):

_5_ Use public bathrooms

_13_ Use public bathroom and wash hands for 15 seconds

_10_ Use bathroom and wash hands for 5 seconds

_9_ Use bathroom and wash hands without reciting alphabet in head

_12_ Touch lock on bathroom door with hands (not sleeve)

_16_ Touch toilet with hands (not toilet paper)

_14_ Touch flusher with hands

_8_ Touch faucet

_6_ Use first paper towel from dispenser

_11_ Touch doorknob or handle of bathroom with hands

_3_ Sit next to someone for one minute after he or she sneezed

_1_ Walk by the pharmacy part of the drugstore

_15_ Have lunch near a sick kid

_4_ Go to a friend's house after the friend was sick last week

_7_ Touch doorknobs and handles in public places

_2_ Go to a friend's house without asking about recent illnesses

After ranking them in order from easiest to hardest, Andrew wrote in all of the steps on his ladder, with the easiest at the bottom and the hardest at the top:

Touch toilet with hands (not toilet paper)

Have lunch near a sick kid

Touch flusher with hands

Use public bathroom and wash hands for 15 seconds

Touch lock on bathroom door with hands

Touch doorknob or handle of bathroom with hands

Use bathroom and wash hands for 5 seconds

Use bathroom and wash hands without reciting alphabet in head

Touch faucet

Touch doorknobs and handles in public places

Use first paper towel from dispenser

Use public bathrooms

Go to a friend's house after the friend was sick last week

Sit next to someone for one minute after he or she sneezed

Go to a friend's house without asking about recent illnesses

Walk by the pharmacy part of the drugstore

Example 2
Alicia, 11 years old,
OCD: Contamination Type

Event: Eat cookie from bake sale

Thought: What if the person who baked it was sick? Now I will get their germs and be sick, too! The eggs could have salmonella in them, or the ingredients could be old and expired! What if I throw up?

Feeling: Very, very anxious!

Action: Ask Mom for reassurance that the cookies were safe. Ask friends if they ate cookies from the bake sale and see how they are feeling. Wait 3 days until I feel sure that I didn't get sick from bake sale cookies.

Like Andrew, Alicia worried constantly about getting contaminated with germs and getting sick. However, her worries centered on getting sick from eating food, particularly spoiled food. She avoided eating food from outside of her home as much as possible, but when she did, she would worry that she would get sick and ask her mom to reassure her that she was OK. She avoided foods that she labeled as "dangerous" because they were foods that people got sick from (they either had been recalled or had been causes of illness in the past, like mad cow disease). Other foods, like grilled cheese and pizza, also made her anxious, although she didn't really know why; they just seemed like foods that might make her sick.

List of avoided situations and OCD-related behaviors:
- ➤ Eat grilled cheese and pizza
- ➤ Eat meat at home without asking questions about it
- ➤ Eat meat from a BBQ at a friend's house
- ➤ Eat meat that has been left out on the counter for 2 hours
- ➤ Eat food from a bake sale
- ➤ Eat sample food in a grocery store
- ➤ Make cookies and eat some raw cookie dough
- ➤ Eat yogurt and drink milk without checking the expiration date
- ➤ Eat expired chips

> ➤ Drink milk that expired 1 day ago, then 2 days ago
> ➤ Don't ask Mom for reassurance
> ➤ Eat tomatoes and spinach
> ➤ Sit next to someone who was recently sick
> ➤ Watch videos of people throwing up and imagine throwing up
> ➤ Eat unwashed grapes

Once Alicia listed her items, she ranked them in order (with 1 being the easiest and 15 being the hardest):

_4_ Eat grilled cheese and pizza

_3_ Eat meat at home without asking questions about it

_7_ Eat meat from a BBQ at a friend's house

_14_ Eat meat that has been left out on the counter for 2 hours

_2_ Eat food from a bake sale

_1_ Eat sample food in a grocery store

_15_ Make cookies and eat some raw cookie dough

_6_ Eat yogurt and drink milk without checking the expiration date

_12_ Eat expired chips

_13_ Drink milk that expired 1 day ago, then 2 days ago

_9_ Don't ask Mom for reassurance

_5_ Eat tomatoes and spinach

_10_ Sit next to someone who was recently sick

_11_ Watch videos of people throwing up and imagine throwing up

_8_ Eat unwashed grapes

After ranking them in order from easiest to hardest, Alicia wrote in all of the steps on her ladder:

Make cookies and eat some raw cookie dough

Eat meat that has been left out on the counter for 2 hours

Drink milk that expired 1 day ago, then 2 days ago

Eat expired chips

Watch videos of people throwing up and imagine throwing up

Sit next to someone who was recently sick

Don't ask Mom for reassurance

Eat unwashed grapes

Eat meat from a BBQ at a friend's house

Eat yogurt and drink milk without checking the expiration date

Eat tomatoes and spinach

Eat grilled cheese and pizza

Eat meat at home without asking questions about it

Eat food from a bake sale

Eat sample food in a grocery store

> **Example 3:**
> Sydney, 10 years old, OCD:
> Doubting/Indecisiveness Types
>
> **Event:** Step on something
>
> **Thought:** What if I stepped on a bug and killed it?
>
> **Feeling:** Very, very anxious!
>
> **Action:** Go back and check sidewalk.

Sydney's OCD caused her to doubt and question many things, including her own actions. She would do something and then feel unsure if she had done it or not. To get rid of this uncomfortable feeling, she would tell her mom the details of her actions, and let her mom be the judge of whether Sydney had done it or not. Sydney also struggled to make decisions and would often get stuck on a meaningless decision for hours. For example, she would stand in front of the kitchen pantry for 40 minutes, unable to decide on which snack to eat.

List of avoided situations and OCD-related behaviors:
➤ Step on pencil on purpose and don't report to Mom
➤ Decide on a snack in 20 minutes, then 10 minutes, then less than 5 minutes
➤ Use the bathroom and step on toilet paper on purpose
➤ Don't tell or confess to Mom 2 days this week, then 3, 5, and 7 days
➤ Decide on what to wear in 5–10 minutes
➤ Decide on what to have for dinner in 2 minutes or less
➤ Decide on whom to make plans with in 5 minutes or less
➤ Decide on whom to sit with at assembly in 3 seconds
➤ State what I did during the day without doubting if it happened
➤ Don't check to see if I stepped on something
➤ Walk through the woods and step on sticks and don't report to Mom
➤ Light a candle and then blow it out without telling Mom

Once Sydney listed her items, she ranked them in order (with 1 being the easiest and 12 being the hardest):

_4_   Step on pencil on purpose and don't report to Mom

_7_   Decide on a snack in 20 minutes, then 10 minutes, then less than 5 minutes

_1_   Use the bathroom and step on toilet paper on purpose

_8_   Don't tell or confess to Mom 2 days this week, then 3, 5, 7 days

_2_   Decide on what to wear in 5-10 minutes

_9_   Decide on what to have for dinner in 2 minutes or less

_6_   Decide on whom to make plans with in 5 minutes or less

_3_   Decide on whom to sit with at assembly in 3 seconds

_11_   State what I did during the day without doubting if it happened

_5_   Don't check to see if I stepped on something

_12_   Walk through the woods and step on sticks and don't report to Mom

_10_   Light a candle and then blow it out without telling Mom

After ranking them in order from easiest to hardest, Sydney wrote in all of the steps on her ladder:

Walk through the woods and step on
sticks and don't report to Mom

State what I did during the day
without doubting if it happened

Light a candle and then blow it out
without telling Mom

Decide on what to have for
dinner in 2 minutes or less

Don't tell or confess to Mom 2 days
this week, then 3, 5, and 7 days

Decide on a snack in 20 minutes, then
10 minutes, then less than 5 minutes

Decide on whom to make plans
with in 5 minutes or less

Don't check to see if I stepped on something

Step on pencil on purpose and
don't report to Mom

Decide on whom to sit with at
assembly in 3 seconds

Decide on what to wear in 5–10 minutes

Use the bathroom and step on
toilet paper on purpose

> **Example 4:**
> Jasmine, 15 years old, OCD:
> Symmetry/"Just Feels Right" Types
>
> **Event:** Look at desk
>
> **Thought:** Things are out of order. They need to be straight.
>
> **Feeling:** Very, very uncomfortable!
>
> **Action:** Order and arrange everything until it is all lined up.

Jasmine struggled to feel comfortable unless things were in order and felt right around her. She spend a good amount of time every day straightening her desk and arranging things in her room until it felt right to her. She couldn't stand having the closet door cracked open, things needed to be perfectly aligned on her desk, with everything facing the right way, and when she slept at night, her covers needed to lie evenly over her. If any of these conditions were not met, Jasmine would feel physically uncomfortable and couldn't relax. When Jasmine walked into a room, she noticed the angles and randomly saw connecting lines, and she couldn't help but focus on making the lines seem straight by connecting them as perfect squares.

List of avoided situations and OCD-related behaviors:
➤ Have 1–2 things that are not perfectly aligned on the desk and leave them there
➤ Have a "messy" desk without fixing it
➤ Sleep over at a friend's house where everything is out of order and "messy"
➤ Leave paper partially sticking out of a folder
➤ Mismatch shoes in closet
➤ Wear two different black socks to school
➤ Walk into room and change straight, square lines to squiggly, crooked ones and draw it
➤ Let brother come in room and move things around without telling me
➤ Stare at a backward-written letter on a piece of paper (such as a backward "R")
➤ Let Dad come in room and put books out of order
➤ Leave backpack zipper partially opened

➤ Sleep with closet door cracked open a bit
➤ Leave closet door open halfway for a whole day
➤ Leave broken pen cap on pen and sticking out of pen holder
➤ Turn 2, then 4, then 8 things around in room
➤ Turn clock upside down on wall and leave it there for one week
➤ Sleep with blanket laid unevenly upon me
➤ Pack an odd number of underwear, shorts, and T-shirts for camp this summer

Once Jasmine listed her items, she ranked them in order (with 1 being the easiest and 18 being the hardest):

_9_ Have 1–2 things that are not perfectly aligned on the desk and leave them there

_5_ Have a "messy" desk without fixing it

_2_ Sleep over at a friend's house where everything is out of order and "messy"

_4_ Leave paper partially sticking out of folder

_7_ Mismatch shoes in closet

_13_ Wear two different black socks to school

_10_ Walk into room and change straight, square lines to squiggly, crooked ones and draw it

_16_ Let brother come in room and move things around without telling me

_8_ Stare at a backward-written letter on a piece of paper (such as a backward "R")

_15_ Let Dad come in room and put books out of order

_1_ Leave backpack zipper partially opened

_11_ Sleep with closet door cracked open a bit

_12_ Leave closet door open halfway for a whole day

_6_ Leave broken pen cap on pen and sticking out of pen holder

__14__ Turn 2, then 4, then 8 things around in room

__18__ Turn clock upside down on wall and leave it there for one week

__17__ Sleep with blanket laid unevenly upon me

__3__ Pack an odd number of underwear, shorts, and T-shirts for camp this summer

After ranking them in order from easiest to hardest, Jasmine wrote in all of the steps on her ladder:

Turn clock upside down on wall and leave it there for one week
Sleep with blanket laid unevenly upon me
Let brother come in room and move things around without telling me
Let Dad come in room and put books out of order
Turn 2, then 4, then 8 things around in room
Wear two different black socks to school
Leave closet door open halfway for a whole day
Sleep with closet door cracked open a bit
Walk into room and change straight, square lines to squiggly, crooked ones and draw it
Have 1–2 things that are not perfectly aligned on desk and leave them there
Stare at a backward-written letter on a piece of paper (such as a backward "R")

Mismatch shoes in closet

Leave broken pen cap on pen and
sticking out of pen holder

Have a "messy" desk without fixing it

Leave paper partially sticking out of folder

Pack an odd number of underwear, shorts,
and T-shirts for camp this summer

Sleep over at a friend's house where
everything is out of order and "messy"

Leave backpack zipper partially opened

Example 5:
William, 16 years old,
OCD: Scrupulosity Type

Event: Asked to go to a party with friends

Thought: I shouldn't have fun or else I will be punished.
Something bad will happen if I enjoy myself and feel
pleasure.

Feeling: Very, very anxious!

Action: Tell my friends that I can't go. Stay home and do
homework instead.

William's OCD led him to feel a strong sense of guilt any time he did something he enjoyed or labeled unnecessary, and the more enjoyable or unnecessary the activity, the guiltier he felt. His OCD held him back from doing things that all of his other friends were able to do, like go out on the weekends and enjoy himself, play video games for hours, and pursue dating girls. He really liked girls, especially one in particular, but could never ask any out because he feared that the guilt would be too strong. In fact, he had never held hands with a girl and certainly never kissed one. Although he had perfect attendance at school and A's in every class, he was not enjoying the feeling of success because his social life was lacking so much. William could not identify a true reason why he felt this way, and he acknowledged that it didn't make sense and was irrational; however, the feeling was so strong that it ruled his life.

List of avoided situations and OCD-related behaviors:

➤ Go to a party on the weekend
➤ Make a plan for all of my friends to go out on a weekend
➤ Go to the movies on a weeknight
➤ Don't do homework on weekend nights (except during exam week)
➤ Talk to a girl for an extended period of time
➤ Ask a girl for her number
➤ Hold hands with a girl
➤ Kiss a girl
➤ Play video games for 2 hours
➤ Invite friends over on a weeknight
➤ Skip school one day and go to the movies (with parents' permission!)
➤ Think about girls I like, even if I start feeling guilty when doing so
➤ Eat three desserts in one night
➤ Go on vacation and miss 2 days of school

Once William listed his items, he ranked them in order (with 1 being the easiest and 14 being the hardest):

__4__ Go to a party on the weekend

__6__ Make a plan for all of my friends to go out on a weekend

__9__ Go to the movies on a weeknight

__1__ Don't do homework on weekend nights (except during exam week)

__7__ Talk to a girl for an extended period of time

__12__ Ask a girl for her number

__13__ Hold hands with a girl

__14__ Kiss a girl

__2__ Play video games for 2 hours

__3__ Invite friends over on a weeknight

__10__ Skip school one day and go to the movies (with parents' permission!)

__5__ Think about girls I like, even if I start feeling guilty when doing so

__8__ Eat three desserts in one night

__11__ Go on vacation with family or friends and miss 2 days of school

After ranking them in order from easiest to hardest, William wrote in all the steps on his ladder:

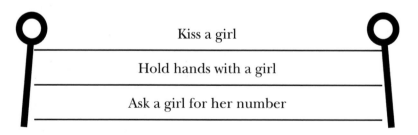

Kiss a girl

Hold hands with a girl

Ask a girl for her number

n with family or friends
ss 2 days of school

ol one day and go to the
(with parents' permission!)

o the movies on a weeknight

Eat 3 desserts in one night

to a girl for an extended period of time

Make a plan for all of my friends to
go out on a weekend

Think about girls you like, even if you
start feeling guilty when doing so

Go to a party on the weekend

Invite friends over on a weeknight

Play video games for 2 hours

Don't do homework on weekend nights
(except during exam week)

Note that William's ladder includes steps that may seem a bit irresponsible (missing school, eating three desserts in one night); however, his steps were designed to address his difficulties with feeling pleasure and enjoyment. This ladder is not a typical example, and William's parents were very supportive of each step on his ladder and knew that it was important for him to do things that he considered "wrong" to challenge his scrupulosity-type OCD.

> **Example 6:**
> Kevin, 14 years old,
> OCD: Scrupulosity Type
>
> **Event:** Walk by a park with other kids playing
>
> **Thought/Urge:** What if I hurt one of those kids or touched their privates? What if someone knew my thoughts? Does thinking it mean that I did it? Is it as bad as doing it?
>
> **Feeling:** Very, very anxious!
>
> **Action:** Shake head four times to the right, quickly and forcefully.

Like William, Kevin worried about doing something bad, even though there was no reason for him to feel like he had done anything wrong (since he hadn't). Kevin's worries were different, though, and had a different theme. Kevin worried about hurting other children, particularly younger ones, and about touching them inappropriately. He never came close to doing this behavior and didn't feel sexual feelings toward younger children; however, he continued to have these unwanted and intrusive thoughts. Kevin was extremely distressed about these thoughts and also very embarrassed that he had them at all.

List of avoided situations and OCD-related behaviors:

➤ Walk by a park
➤ Walk by a school playground
➤ Talk to younger children
➤ Play with younger children
➤ Babysit younger cousins
➤ Read about sexual predators
➤ Have thoughts without shaking head at all
➤ Read *My Body Is Private* or similar book for children about private parts
➤ Talk to parents about thoughts
➤ Think about lighting a candle and then light one (to show the difference between thought and action)
➤ Think about winning a million dollars (to show the difference between thought and action)

Once Kevin listed his items, he ranked them in order (with 1 being the easiest and 11 being the hardest):

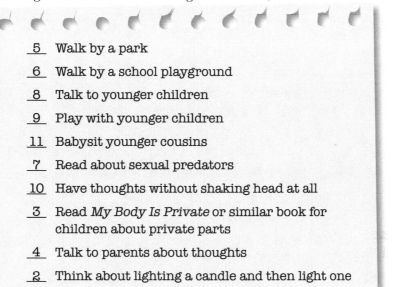

_5_ Walk by a park

_6_ Walk by a school playground

_8_ Talk to younger children

_9_ Play with younger children

_11_ Babysit younger cousins

_7_ Read about sexual predators

_10_ Have thoughts without shaking head at all

_3_ Read _My Body Is Private_ or similar book for children about private parts

_4_ Talk to parents about thoughts

_2_ Think about lighting a candle and then light one

_1_ Think about winning a million dollars

After ranking them in order from easiest to hardest, Kevin wrote in all the steps on his ladder:

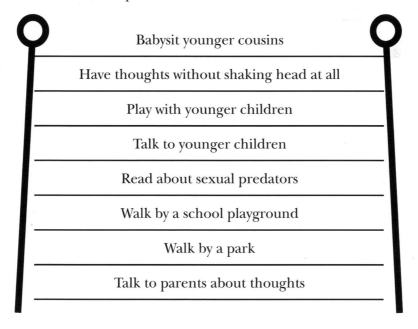

Babysit younger cousins

Have thoughts without shaking head at all

Play with younger children

Talk to younger children

Read about sexual predators

Walk by a school playground

Walk by a park

Talk to parents about thoughts

Read *My Body Is Private* or similar book for children about private parts
Think about lighting a candle and then light one
Think about winning a million dollars

Hopefully, by reviewing the six examples above and seeing the process of creating the ladders, you are starting to have some ideas about what you want to include in your own ladder. Again, it is very important to go ahead and make your ladder now. Good luck!

What I Know Now

This chapter focused on explaining the process of making your ladder, which is the goal-setting part of the program. We reviewed the six cases of OCD introduced in Chapter 1, and you saw how each student's ladder was developed.

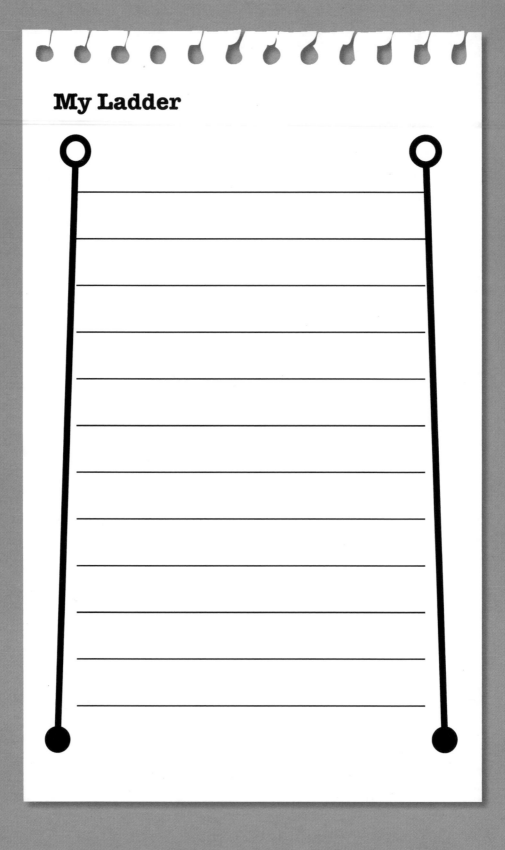

My Ladder

CHAPTER 4

LEARNING HOW TO RELAX

"Learning how to be able to sit and relax took a while for me. I had to practice every day and mostly listened to the relaxing scripts with music in the background. I used to squirm around a lot and keep my eyes open, but now I lie still and keep my eyes closed. Practicing paid off, and now I know how to calm down and really relax."

—Ben, age 12

To help you prepare for facing your fears and taking the steps on your ladder, this chapter will teach you several different relaxation techniques. This chapter addresses the "body" part of anxiety, or the physical symptoms of stress and discomfort that are linked to your OCD.

Some kids have a hard time with recognizing when their bodies feel stressed or anxious. As discussed in Chapter 1, common body symptoms include the following:

➤ muscle tension,
➤ shallow breathing (breathing that only goes in your upper chest instead of traveling all the way down to your lower belly),
➤ fast heartbeat,
➤ stomachaches,
➤ sweaty palms,
➤ feeling dizzy or lightheaded, and
➤ hot flushes.

There are other physical symptoms that could be associated with anxiety from OCD, and every person's body is different.

It is important to know that there is a mind-body connection, meaning that your mind affects your body and your body affects your mind. For example, if the fire alarm goes off at school, your mind registers the alarm and thinks, "Fire! I better get outside!" This causes your body to have a *fight-or-flight* reaction as it prepares either to run or to protect itself. When this happens, your heartbeat gets fast, blood flows into your legs, and your body temperature rises. Your body and mind work together and influence one another. Similarly, if you have a positive attitude about your body and your health, you will likely get sick less often. If you worry about your health and think of your body as fragile, you may be more likely to get hurt or injured. Many times, if you *think* it, your body will *feel* it.

It is important to understand this mind-body connection, because it relates to your OCD. When your OCD is triggered, your mind is registering that there is a threat or something to be worried or alerted about, and then your body will have a hard time being relaxed. The steps on your ladder represent difficult situations

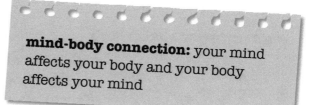

mind-body connection: your mind affects your body and your body affects your mind

that you tend to avoid, and you likely avoid them because they are so unpleasant and uncomfortable for you. Also, you probably don't *feel* that good when in those situations. Right now, because you have spent a long time either avoiding those situations or dealing with them while feeling very uncomfortable, those situations have been associated with anxiety for you. So, whenever you try to face those situations, it will be hard to do at first. Relaxation is one way that will help you cope, or deal with, the discomfort that you feel when facing your fears.

Sometimes you will be able to actually relax in such situations, although this will probably not happen during the first few times you practice. Sometimes, however, you will feel so uncomfortable that the purpose of relaxation will simply be to help you better handle or deal with the discomfort, rather than getting completely calm.

The most important thing to keep in mind is that you need to practice these relaxation techniques while you are relatively calm, *not* when you are upset or anxious. The goal is to really learn how to relax and become a master at relaxing, so when you are anxious, you will be able to calm down. But if you practice only during times of anxiety, relaxation may not work as well.

There are several ways to calm the body, and this chapter will focus on five:

1. Calm breathing

2. Progressive muscle relaxation
3. Relaxing imagery
4. Mindfulness meditation
5. Yoga

The best approach is to practice them all, and then pick one or two that work best for you and use those during the exposure phase. You can practice on your own or have your parent help you in the process. Try to practice calm breathing every day, and then add one of the other techniques, trying a different technique each day until you figure out which one(s) work best for you.

CALM BREATHING

Calm breathing is a great technique, and most kids love it. There are two types:
1. Lower diaphragmatic breathing (traditional calm breathing), and
2. One-nostril breathing.

LOWER DIAPHRAGMATIC BREATHING (TRADITIONAL CALM BREATHING)

Your diaphragm is a sheet of muscle wall located just under your ribs, and it is a major muscle used during breathing. "Lower diaphragmatic breathing" refers to breathing in which the breath goes all the way down into the lower part of stomach, below your diaphragm. The goal is for the air to travel all the way down into the lower part of your belly, near your belly button. When you are nervous or scared, your breath only goes into the top of your chest, but when you are

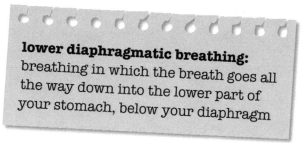

lower diaphragmatic breathing: breathing in which the breath goes all the way down into the lower part of your stomach, below your diaphragm

calm or relaxed, your breath travels farther down into your lower abdomen.

The best way to practice this is to lie down on the floor or a bed. Gently breathe in (inhale) through your nose for about 4 seconds, hold the breath for 4 seconds, and then slowly breathe out (exhale) through your nose for 4 seconds. To help remember to breathe in through your nose and out through your mouth, think: *smell the roses, blow out the candles.*

When you are lying down, imagine that the top of your chest is the shallow end of the pool and that the bottom of your stomach, near your belly button, is the deep end of the pool. You want the air to travel all the way down into the deep end. Look down at your belly and try to get the breath to "balloon out" the lower part of it. Don't push out the lower part; let the breath cause it to rise and fall. Remember to breathe in and out very slowly.

Another way to master this technique: place a foam block (like the ones used in yoga) or a lightweight stuffed animal on your upper chest. Pretend to breathe in an anxious way, only in your upper chest, and watch the block or stuffed animal move up and down. Now try to keep the block or stuffed animal still by doing lower diaphragmatic breathing and letting the air go all the way down to your lower stomach—the block will stay still but your lower belly will rise and fall as you breathe in and out.

If you are having a hard time doing this type of breathing, try using a 10-pound sandbag (another type of yoga prop) and put that on your upper chest instead. Because it weighs so much, the sandbag will make it very hard for you to breathe with your upper chest; it will make you breathe in a calm way. Instead of a sandbag, you could use a big bag of rice or a phonebook. Just make sure that you ask your parents first, and make sure they agree that what you are using won't hurt you; in fact, it's best to have a parent watch you as you do it.

Many kids who come to see me have "learned" calm breathing in the past, yet when I ask them to show me, I see that they really haven't learned how to do it correctly. It requires practice, and by using the props (block/stuffed animal, sandbag/bag of rice), you will really understand what to do. With practice, you will be able to know when your breathing is calm versus when it is anxious.

ONE-NOSTRIL BREATHING

One-nostril breathing is wonderful and really forces your body to have a slow, calm breath. The goal is to do this kind of breathing for 3–5 minutes. When you do it for a full 3–5 minutes, you will really start to see the benefits.

Use your finger to hold one of your nostrils closed, and then close your mouth. Breathe very, very slowly in and out through only one nostril.

First, breathe in through one nostril for 6 seconds, then out through the same nostril for 6 seconds. Then do it again, but this time take 8 seconds to breathe in and 8 seconds to breathe out. Then, if you can, do it again and take 10 seconds to breathe in and 10 seconds to breathe out.

You can breathe in and out through the same nostril or breathe in through one nostril and then switch and breathe out through the other. The most important part is that you are breathing in or breathing out through only one nostril at a time (while closing the other nostril and closing your mouth). Also, a lot of kids find it helpful to let out a big breath (sort of like a deep sigh) before they start the calm breathing, as this allows them to have more air to breathe in through their nostril.

PROGRESSIVE MUSCLE RELAXATION

Progressive muscle relaxation (PMR) involves making your muscles relax by first tightening them up and holding them for about 5–10 seconds. You do one section of your body at a time, starting with your hands and going all the way down to your feet. When you use the steps below, pay attention to what your body feels like

progressive muscle relaxation (PMR): making your muscles relax by first tightening them up and holding them for about 5–10 seconds, then letting them relax again

when your muscles are tight and tense and when they are loose and relaxed.

Find a comfortable place to sit, and do the following 10 steps:

1. *Hands*: Make tight fists, imagining that you are squeezing the juice out of a lemon. Hold your fists nice and tight and count to 10. Then let go and shake them out to loosen them up.

2. *Arms*: Now pull your arms into your body, almost pushing them into your ribs. Tighten up your biceps, triceps, and forearm muscles (all of the muscles in your arms above and below your elbows), but don't make fists or tighten your hands. Hold it for 1, 2, 3, 4, 5, 6, 7, 8, 9, and 10, then let go and shake your arms out. Remember to notice what the muscles feel like when they are tense and when they are loose. Sometimes once you loosen them, your muscles will feel a little tingly. This is totally normal.

3. *Shoulders*: Bring your shoulders all the way up toward your ears and tighten them up; this also should make the back of your neck tight. Hold it for the count of 10, then allow your shoulders to drop down toward your hips. As you do this, say the word "relax" to yourself and breathe out slowly through your mouth.

4. *Back*: Now pull your shoulders back and arch your back in toward your chest. Imagine that there is a string connected to your chest and someone is pulling the string up, lifting your chest up toward the ceiling. This will tighten your back. Hold it for 10, then let it go and feel the difference between tension and relaxation.

5. *Stomach*: Squeeze and pull your stomach, or abdominal, muscles in toward your spine. Say "hut," like the noise football players make before they snap, or hike, the ball, and hold it in. Keep it tight for 10 seconds, then let it go.

6. *Buttocks*: Now squeeze your buttocks (muscles in you butt—they are important, too!). Hold for 10 seconds, then let go and loosen them up. Try not to tighten your legs when doing this—just keep it specific to your buttocks muscles.

7. *Legs (toes in)*: Stick your legs and feet straight out in front of you and point your toes in toward your chest. This will tighten the muscles in your legs and thighs. Make the muscles as tight as you can and hold for 10 seconds, then let go and allow your legs to gently drop to the ground and relax.

8. *Legs (toes out)*: Stick your legs and feet straight out in front of you again, but this time, point your toes straight out away from you and tighten up the muscles in your legs, thighs, and feet. Try to get it so you feel a little cramping in the bottom of your feet. Hold for 10 seconds, then let go, allowing your legs to gently drop to the floor.

9. *Face*: Now, tighten up all of the muscles in your face. Start by clenching your teeth and jaw. Then squish up your nose, lifting it up, and then close your eyes and squeeze the muscles around them, tightening up your forehead. Hold this tightness in your whole face for 10 seconds, then let go and relax. Open your mouth a little bit and move your jaw from left to right and then in circles. This will allow the jaw to become even more relaxed.

10. *Whole Body*: You want to go from being a stiff, tight **robot** to being a loose, relaxed **rag doll**! Start with tight fists, then add arms, then bring your shoulders up to your ears, then pull them back to tighten your back, then squeeze your stomach into your spine, then tighten your buttocks, then put your legs out in front of you with your toes pointing away from you and cramp up your feet, and then tighten your jaw and whole face. Hold for 10 seconds (robot) and then let go (rag doll), loosening every muscle in your body. I could tell that you were a really relaxed rag doll if I tried to lift up your arm and it felt very heavy and loose.

RELAXING IMAGERY

Relaxing imagery is another way to relax your body and mind. Find a comfortable place to sit or lie down. You can make yourself more comfortable by using pillows or arranging blankets to have more support under your head and under your knees. You also may enjoy listening to some relaxing music (with no words) in the background.

You can either read the scene yourself, or have a parent or someone else read it to you. Just make sure they use their best calming voice, and that they don't read it too quickly. I recommend that either you or your parent make a recording of one of the scripts below, and then you can replay the recording and listen to it regularly.

Here is the first relaxing imagery script.

Once you are comfortable, **close your eyes and take a deep breath in through your nose and out through your mouth.** As you breathe in, imagine that you are breathing in clean, relaxing air, and as you breathe out, let go of any stress or tension that you might be holding onto. Breathing in, let the calm air go all the way down to the bottom of your belly. Breathing out, let go of the air so your belly becomes flat. With each breath, you feel more and more relaxed.

This is your time for relaxation, and you have nowhere to go and nothing to do. If any thoughts come into your mind, that is perfectly fine. Just let them flow by without focusing on them. Anything important will come back to you after the relaxation.

Imagine that you are visiting a beautiful lake, and picture yourself sitting or standing close to the water. Your body feels so comfortable and calm. It is a perfect day and the temperature is just right—not too hot, and there is a soothing breeze that you feel especially on your face. You notice that your body begins to loosen up.

Look at the water—notice how peaceful the water is. You can hear the sound of the water as it hits up against the land. You love the sound that the water makes as it keeps rocking up and down, back and forth, against the land. The rhythm of the water coming in and out toward the land is very soothing, and you notice your attention is locked onto the water. The more your watch the water, the calmer you feel. You begin to feel your muscles loosen and your breathing slow down. You feel very, very calm. Watching the water is soothing and calming.

The breeze is making slight waves on the surface of the water, and you love watching these waves flowing in, then flowing out, and then just flowing along. Nature is very peaceful. You can trust nature and feel yourself being held by the beauty around you.

Lying on the grass next to the lake, you think more about these waves. You imagine a wave coming over your body, and as it does, it soothes and comforts you. The wave slowly goes over your toes, feet, and ankles. Then it goes up your legs, knees, and thighs. It goes over your hips, hands, arms, stomach, and chest and all the way up to your shoulders, just up to your neck. The wave is warm and comforting. It hangs out for just a minute, relaxing and soothing all of your muscles. Then the wave begins to leave, taking away all remaining tension, going down your chest, stomach, arms, hands, and hips, all the way down past your thighs, knees, legs, and ankles, and then finally leaving your feet and toes. You are now even more relaxed, and your body feels light and loose.

Looking back toward the lake, you see magnificent mountains in the distance. The mountains are strong, and you enjoy looking at them and thinking about just how amazing they are. There are some white clouds looming around the tops of the mountains, set against the background of a bright blue sky. Again, you are in a state of deep peace and inner calmness.

(pause for a moment)

You notice the sounds of birds singing and the sounds of the wind blowing, and you love the feeling of being surrounded by nature. You see trees near the lake, and their leaves are swaying back and forth as the breeze comes and goes. Be fully aware of this moment and of all the things you are seeing, hearing, and feeling. Notice how your body feels. Take a moment to enjoy this relaxation, noticing how calm and slow your breathing is. Stay here as long as you'd like.

(pause for several minutes and enjoy this relaxed state)

In just a minute, count to 10, and imagine that you are climbing up a set of stairs. With each step, you become more and more alert, but still very relaxed. At the top of the stairs, there will be an archway. You will walk through the archway, and then you will be back in your own room, keeping the feelings of relaxation within you.

One, take the first step.

Two, take the second step.

Three, take the third step.

Four, take the fourth step.

Five, take the fifth step.

> Six, take the sixth step.
> Seven, take the seventh step.
> Eight, take the eighth step.
> Nine, take the ninth step.
> And ten, take the tenth step.
>
> Walk through the archway, and you are back in your room. Remind yourself that you can become this relaxed anytime you'd like, and it will only take 5 minutes!

You can practice relaxing imagery with this or any other relaxing scene. You can ask your parent to make up a scene for you, or you can create one yourself. It can be anywhere you'd like—it can be a real place, such as a special place that you have traveled to, one you have seen in a movie, or a made-up one. The only rule is that this place needs to be free of stress and completely relaxing to you.

You either can stop here and skip ahead to the section on mindfulness meditation, or you can read through the additional script below.

An alternative relaxing imagery scene follows that you can use instead of, or in addition to, the lake scene above. Again, either you or your parent can make a recording for you to listen to when practicing relaxation.

> Once you are comfortable, **close your eyes and take a deep breath in through your nose and out through your mouth.** As you breathe in, imagine that you are breathing in clean, relaxing air, and as you breathe out, let go of any stress or tension that you might be holding on to. Breathing in, let the calm air go all the way down to the bottom of your belly. Breathing out, let go of the air so your belly becomes flat. With each breath, you feel more and more relaxed.
>
> This is your time for relaxation, and you have nowhere to go and nothing to do. If any thoughts come into your mind, that is perfectly fine. Just let them flow by without focusing on them. Anything important will come back to you after the relaxation.
>
> **Imagine** that you are in a beautiful field. This field is a very safe and relaxing place. The field is vast and wide, and you can see everything

clearly around you. Part of the field is lined with wheat, and you notice how the wind softly blows the tips of the wheat and how relaxing this is to watch. Another part of the field is a large stretch of green grass, and there are several big, beautiful trees. Two of the trees have a hammock stretched between them.

You look out into the field and notice that your whole body feels calm. You have a feeling of being held and comforted. You can feel the sun shining down upon you, warming your body. The air is the perfect temperature, and the sky is blue with white, cottony clouds.

You move closer to the wheat grass and notice its lovely colors, with the sunlight causing the tips to glisten as they sway from the breeze. The smell is fresh and natural. You run your fingers over the top of the grass, feeling how soft and light it is. You swing both of your hands out in front of you, along the top edges of the grass. You are standing tall, but relaxed. You feel lightness and confidence in your body. You feel clear in your body, free of tension. You close your eyes for a moment, feeling the sunlight warming your face. You breathe in and out calmly and become even more relaxed.

(pause for a moment)

Looking at the trees, you are reminded of how strong the Earth is. You can imagine the roots of the trees and how far down they go, securing their position in the Earth. You feel the strength of the trees, and this makes you feel safe and secure. You walk toward the trees and decide to settle into the hammock. Sitting down, you swing one leg up onto the hammock and then the other. This hammock is so comfortable and relaxing. You lie back and your body sways from left to right, left to right. You look up at the tops of the trees and see the leaves swaying from the wind. You hear birds in the background, including an owl—whooo, whooo, whooo. You love how the owl sounds, and you are so relaxed that you gently close your eyes and just enjoy the calm swaying back and forth, back and forth. Sunlight streams through the tops of the trees and moves through the leaves and branches, causing patches of sunlight to rest upon your body, providing you with additional warmth. You are so content. You are so calm.

(pause for a moment)

Be fully aware of this moment, and all of the things you are seeing, hearing, and feeling. Notice how your body feels. Take a moment to enjoy this relaxation, noticing how calm and slow your breathing is. Stay here as long as you'd like.

(pause for several minutes and enjoy relaxed state)

In just a minute, count to 10, and imagine that you are climbing up a set of stairs. With each step, you become more and more alert, but still very relaxed. At the top of the stairs, there will be an archway. You will walk through the archway, and then you will be back in your own room, keeping the feelings of relaxation within you.

One, take the first step.

Two, take the second step.

Three, take the third step.

Four, take the fourth step.

Five, take the fifth step.

Six, take the sixth step.

Seven, take the seventh step.

Eight, take the eighth step.

Nine, take the ninth step.

And ten, take the tenth step.

Walk through the archway, and you are back in your room. Remind yourself that you can become this relaxed anytime you'd like, and it will only take 5 minutes!

MINDFULNESS MEDITATION

Of all the different ways to relax your body and mind, meditation is very useful in helping you "stay with" the uncomfortable feelings of anxiety, which is important to be able to do when doing the exposures. There are many different types of meditation; the one you will learn here is called "mindfulness meditation."

The term *mindfulness* was introduced to you in Chapter 2, where it was explained that mindfulness refers to a different way of experiencing yourself and the mind. It involves being fully aware in the present moment, the exact moment that you are in right now. When you can truly be in the present moment, you will see that you are totally OK. No matter what you might be upset about from the past, or what you are worried about for the future, you are completely fine in the present moment. Nothing bad is happening to you in this moment; even though anxiety might make you *feel* this way (because anxiety signals a threat), nothing bad is actually happening to you.

Mindfulness is being fully aware of yourself and your thoughts, but in a way that allows you to be less reactive to them. For example, you might notice that you are feeling anxious and are uncomfortable, yet by *noticing* it, you will tend to be a bit separated, or distanced, from it, and then will be less likely to *react* to it. It is as if you become an observer of your anxiety and discomfort.

When dealing with OCD, the goal is to be fully aware of when you are being triggered into OCD thoughts and what those thoughts are. It is easy to feel that the OCD is just the way you are or is just a typical part of your life. Being mindful will allow you to be more aware of your OCD, how it comes out in your life, and how it makes you feel.

The concept of mindfulness is new to most kids and teens. Even if you don't fully "get it," it is great that you are beginning to know about it, as then it will be something you fully understand in the future.

Learning how to *be mindful* is the fundamental skill of mindfulness meditation. When you are mindful, you are really experiencing the present moment, and this is necessary when practicing mediation.

The more often you practice, the more it will start to come naturally to you. Some kids will find it pretty easy to get out of their thinking mind, while others will find it very difficult and will need more practice. Either way, just be confident that you will be able to achieve this skill. Try not to judge yourself or the process itself. There is no such thing as "doing it right" because it's not about *doing* anything; rather, it's about simply being. Start with a 5–10 minute practice session each day (right before bed is a great time because you want to wind down anyway, and this practice will help), and gradually build up to a longer practice, such as 20–30 minutes.

MINDFULNESS MEDITATION PRACTICE

Find a comfortable place to sit or lie down. You can choose to close your eyes or keep them open. Focus your attention on the present moment. Just "be" in the moment that you are in. This is not something that should feel like effort, or like something you are trying to do; rather allow your natural state of being just to happen. You were born into a state of awareness and full consciousness, so by doing this, you are really going back to basics.

If you find yourself thinking of something, just note that you are having a thought, and allow yourself to move on. Allow the thought to float on by—don't hold onto it or push it away—just let it float on by you.

Bring your focus to your breath. Feel your lower belly and how it goes up and down with each incoming and outgoing breath. Ground yourself in your breath. Now extend your awareness throughout your body. Feel the support of the chair or the floor below you. Be fully aware of your body.

Now extend your awareness to the space around you. Feel the energy of the space in the room you are in and extend your awareness throughout the room.

Now expand your awareness to outside of the room. Imagine that you are spreading your awareness to beyond the room, into the outside space around you.

Notice the sounds and vibrations around you. Allow those sounds to become a part of your field of awareness. Just observe what you observe.

Again, if any thoughts come into your mind, just let them pass. Don't do anything with them—don't hold onto them or try to push them away. Just stay with the moment you are in. Just sit there in awareness, letting yourself simply be in your natural state.

Note: When doing this, it may feel like you are doing nothing, and to some extent, that is exactly what you are doing; however, the practice of doing nothing and having a clear mind allows you to experience anxiety-free states and know what it feels like to not be consumed with OCD thoughts.

YOGA

Yoga is a form of exercise that greatly helps your body and mind. There are many different types of yoga, but the goal of most types is to help you gain more balance and strength in your body and bring harmony to your body and mind. Recent research shows that yoga is beneficial for improving psychological problems, including anxiety and stress.

Taking a yoga class or watching a yoga video is the best way to learn the poses and to make sure you do them correctly without getting injured.

Below are three popular poses that are pretty easy to learn and very safe to do. The more you practice, the better you will become at getting the most out of these poses.

1. Standing Mountain Pose

Stand with your feet together (big toes touching) and your arms down by your sides. Stand up nice and tall and very straight with your shoulders back. Try to get your chest to lift up, as if someone is pulling your chest up with a string that is attached to it.

Now turn your palms facing out, away from you. Slowly raise your arms, keeping your elbows straight if you can. Once your arms are all the way up, your hands will be facing one another, and your fingers will be reaching up toward the sky. Stretch up and reach up as high as you can, while keeping your feet planted firmly into the floor. Try to encourage your upper spine to move into your body and your shoulder blades to move closer together.

Continue to reach up with your fingertips, and push your feet down into the floor, as if your feet were the roots of a tree (your leg muscles should become tight as you do this). Your upper body is stretching up while your lower body is pushing down. As you do this, feel confident about yourself and feel your body opening and lengthening as you stretch and stretch.

2. Downward-Facing Dog Pose

Lie facedown on the floor, bend your elbows, and put your hands down on the floor next to your armpits (or chest).

1. Now get up on all fours (on your hands and knees) and spread your fingers apart, but keep your hands with open palms on the floor.
2. Now lift up onto your feet, standing mainly on your toes, lifting your hips up, and keeping your hands on the floor. Your hands should be shoulder-width apart.
3. Continue to lift your hips up and stretch your back. Continue to spread your fingers apart and push your hands against the floor to encourage more lengthening in your spine and more lift in your hips. Hips up, hips up. Feel the stretch.
4. Very good! Now gently come back down onto all fours, lie back down on your stomach, and relax.

3. Child's Pose

Lie facedown on the floor, and touch your big toes together while sitting on the heels of your feet.

1. Now spread your knees apart so your knees go out toward the side.
2. Lay your chest on the floor and let your belly sink down toward the floor as well. Your thighs and knees should be out to the side.
3. Stretch your arms and fingers out in front of you with your arms lifting up a few inches above the floor and your

fingertips touching the floor. As you do this, try to get your upper back and upper spine to come into your body. Feel the stretch.

4. Now bring your arms down by your sides, with your hands (palms facing up) resting on the floor alongside or below your feet. Just let your entire body relax and rest. Let go of any tension in your body.

What I Know Now

This chapter focused on teaching you several different ways to relax. You learned calm breathing, including lower diaphragmatic breathing and one-nostril breathing; progressive muscle relaxation; relaxing imagery; mindfulness meditation; and several yoga poses. Each of these techniques was explained, and you are reminded to practice each technique, with the goal of identifying one or two that work really well and will be useful for you during the exposure/practice phase.

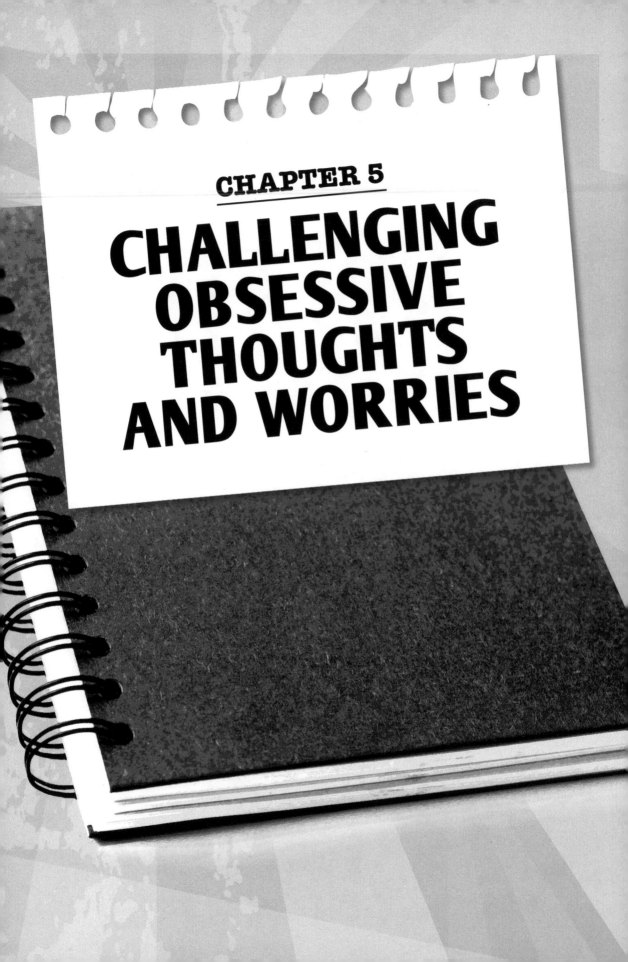

CHAPTER 5

CHALLENGING OBSESSIVE THOUGHTS AND WORRIES

"It was hard to struggle with OCD and all my OCD thoughts that made me doubt everything. I felt unsure of everything and even had a hard time answering simple questions that my friends would ask. Once I figured out how to talk back to my OCD and make myself answer anyway—even when I didn't feel sure—things started to get better."

—Sydney, age 10

Although all of the chapters in this book are important in helping you take control of OCD, this chapter is the most necessary to your success in doing so. This chapter focuses on helping you challenge the thoughts and worries that come from OCD; therefore, this chapter is about the *thoughts* part of anxiety.

OCD CYCLE

In review of the OCD cycle, there is an event (trigger situation) followed by an obsessive thought (which tends to be a thinking error), and then the person feels anxious. To cope with the anxiety, there is a compulsive behavior or ritual (action). Obsessive thoughts can come up in many forms, including repetitive ideas, doubts, questioning, and disturbing images.

IDENTIFYING YOUR OCD THOUGHTS: WHEN MY OCD TALKS, IT SAYS . . .

It is important to identify your own OCD-driven thoughts, not only in order to externalize the OCD, but also to know what thoughts to challenge. As explained in Chapter 2, externalizing the OCD means that you clearly see what OCD is causing you to think. Therefore, you see it as something separate from yourself: Rather than considering the OCD thoughts to be just your own thoughts, you are able to identify those thoughts as symptoms of the disorder.

To help you complete the section below, let's go through a few of the examples of children with OCD to show how they completed the exercise on identifying their OCD thoughts.

Andrew, 12 Years Old: Contamination Type

When Andrew's OCD talked, it said . . .
➤ "Bathrooms are dangerous, and there are dangerous germs in there."
➤ "If I touch the toilet, I will get contaminated and sick."
➤ "If I touch the faucet, I will get someone's germs and might not know it."
➤ "I can prevent getting sick if I am very careful when using bathrooms."
➤ "You have to go through the whole alphabet to wash your hands well enough."
➤ "It is dangerous to be near people who are sick."

Sydney, 10 Years Old: Doubting/Indecisiveness Types

When Sydney's OCD talked, it said . . .
➤ "What if I stepped on a pencil?"
➤ "If I tell Mom everything I did, then I will feel better."
➤ "I should only wear clothes that feel completely right to wear."
➤ "I shouldn't make a mistake."
➤ "There is a right decision and a wrong decision. I will know it's right when it feels right to me."
➤ "I shouldn't upset my friends or disappoint anyone."
➤ "What if the toilet paper touched the floor in the bathroom?"
➤ "What if I stepped on an animal? I felt like I stepped on something. I better go back and check."

William, 16 Years Old: Scrupulosity Type

When William's OCD talked, it said . . .
➤ "Having fun increases the chances that I will be punished."
➤ "Something bad will happen if I enjoy myself and feel pleasure."
➤ "It is safer to stay home and do homework."

➤ "I have to be careful and not take risks. I need to be in control"

➤ "I shouldn't go out on school nights."

➤ "Scheduling or organizing plans with friends makes it worse; then I am responsible for the fun. It's better if someone else arranges the plans."

Using the space below, or on a separate sheet of paper, make a list of what your OCD says when it is triggered.

When my OCD talks, it says . . .

MASTERING YOUR WORRIES

Worries are thoughts, usually about something bad that might happen, that make you feel anxious. When you have OCD, it becomes particularly difficult to break the cycle of obsessive worrying. This is called "rumination," which refers to the process of getting stuck on thinking about worry thoughts. When you ruminate, you have the same worry thoughts going through your mind over and over, and you find it hard to stop focusing on them. There are several ways to challenge your worries, and the goal is to figure out which one(s) work best for you. In addition, Chapter 6 focuses on uncertainty training, and this practice also is very useful in helping you deal with repetitive worries.

rumination: getting stuck on thinking about worry thoughts; when you ruminate, you have the same worry thoughts going through your mind over and over

REFRAME YOUR WORRIES

Reframe your worries by finding a different way of thinking about them. For example, a client with obsessive worries had a fear of having an allergic reaction to nuts, even though he was not allergic at all. He avoided nuts and would ruminate for hours after meals (especially after eating in a restaurant or at someone else's home), worrying that he might have eaten nuts without knowing it and would have an allergic reaction. In challenging his worries, he learned to remind himself that he was not allergic (realistic thinking) and told himself that he could've picked lettuce to be afraid of (because that was another food that he was not allergic to but one he was not afraid of). Then, during the exposure phase when he was eating nuts, he told himself, "It's just lettuce. To my body, it's the same as if I was eating lettuce." This kind of cognitive (or mental) reframe helped him undo and weaken his worries and also allowed him to do the exposures and not let the worries control his behavior.

Another way to reframe your worries is to label them as "useful" or "useless" and then decide on what to do. If it's a *useful* worry (for example, I'm worried about not being prepared enough for my test tomorrow), then you can channel the worry into action and use it to your advantage (for example, study harder for your test). Useful worry can help you be more productive, and it usually doesn't involve a negative physiological anxious reaction. *Useless* worry, on the other hand, generally makes you less productive and usually causes physiological stress. For useless worries, your best bet is to label the worry as useless and either use distraction or mindfulness to deal with it.

Distraction. Use distraction to take your attention away from the worry and put your focus on something else. For example, it can be

distraction: doing something to take your attention away from the worry and bring your focus to something else

playing a mind game such as using the alphabet to come up with lists (for example, *boys' names*: Andre, Brian, Cole, David, Evan, Fred, Gabe, Henry, Isaac, etc.; *jobs*: Artist, Baker, Chemist, Dentist, Engineer, Geographer, Horticulturist, Inventor, etc.) or making your own lists (for example, five things that are green, five things in my backpack, my five favorite songs or movies).

Mindfulness. Using mindfulness to deal with worries involves being aware and acknowledging that you are worrying, and being able to accept this as your experience. This acceptance will make worrying easier to deal with and decrease your tendency to react to the worries. It is as simple as saying to yourself, "I am worried right now, and this is what I tend to do at times. I see that I am worrying and that this is causing me to feel uncomfortable in my body and to have a general feeling of uneasiness." Also, mindfulness encourages you to focus on the present moment and just *be* in the present moment at hand. In the present moment, you will see that you are OK and that nothing bad is happening to you. Anxious thinking makes you *feel like* something bad is happening; however, anxious thinking is not an accurate description of what is happening to you now, rather it is about fears of what *might* happen or what *might have* happened. You also practice mindfulness meditation to become skilled at being in the present moment and suspending your thoughts (for example, being in a thoughtless, relaxed state). Finally, you also can use the other relaxation techniques to help cope with worries.

WORRY TAPES

Make a worry tape (also called an "endless loop tape"; see Chapter 8 for more details on making such a tape) and listen to it during your scheduled "worry time." Set aside a time each day to worry, and try to postpone your worrying throughout the day until this set time. If you tend to worry much of the time and find it hard to control your worries, you may benefit from recording a worry tape. To make a worry tape, record a sampling of what the worries sound like (how you hear them) in your mind. Try to make a 5–10 minute recording, then listen to it over and over for a total of 15–20 minutes a day. This will allow you to become desensitized, or used to, the worry thoughts. For example, the following is a sample from Alicia's worry tape:

What if the milk in my cereal was bad? What if the date was wrong on the carton and it was really expired and I will get sick? What if those cookies were cooked with bad eggs? I will get salmonella and throw up. I will need to wait 48 hours to see if I am OK. I won't know until 48 hours have passed, because that's when salmonella comes out. Maybe Mom knows that milk was expired but is afraid to tell me because I will worry. Mom looked a little worried earlier today. Probably because the milk was expired. Maybe I feel a little sick. Yes, my stomach feels a little nauseous. Oh, no! I'm probably sick with salmonella. I better check the milk again and ask Mom about it and the cookies. Now I will miss school this week and get behind on my work. Like my friend Amber who missed 3 days last week because she was sick.

*Maybe I got sick from her—I did sit next to her last week at lunch.
I might have caught what she caught.*

As you can see, Alicia recorded the tape as her thoughts sounded to her in her mind. Alicia listened to her tape two times in a row each day after school, during her "worry time." This allowed her to become used to hearing herself worry and to the thoughts themselves. After a few weeks of listening to her tape daily, this practice caused her to worry less. When she started worrying as usual, she would recall what she sounded like when she worried, and this caused her to externalize her worries and minimize their strength. She also postponed worrying until her worry time, so when she started thinking a worry thought during the day, she would tell herself, "Save it until later." If the thought kept popping up in her mind, she would make a little note in her assignment book to herself to include that worry later on during worry time.

Ask yourself two things when you are worried:
1. What is the worst thing that could happen?
2. Could I handle it?

Keep in mind that the answer to the second question is *always* "yes." You can handle whatever comes your way and can work through any situation, even the most difficult and scary ones. There is nothing that you cannot handle! Recognize that even though worry is just the anxiety talking to you, you could actually manage any situation.

DETACHED MINDFULNESS

Use the **detached mindfulness** technique (part of metacognitive therapy, as described in Chapter 2) to identify your worries as "just thoughts." This allows you to see that whatever you are thinking about, whether it is true or not, is just a thought. For example, when Alicia would think, "I will get salmonella and throw up," she used detached mindfulness and told herself, "That is just a thought. I see that is just a thought, just like reading is just reading, running is just running, thinking is just thinking. Thinking is just thinking; no matter what I am thinking about, it is still *only* thinking. And because it is only thinking, I can put off checking right now."

In detached mindfulness, you don't try to actually change the thought—you just try to change how you experience the thought, making it something you can observe yourself doing, rather than something you respond to. With practice, this will be a skill you have command of, though at first it might seem hard to do. Once you figure out how to do it, it will come more naturally and easily.

ATTENTION TRAINING TECHNIQUE

Use the **attention training technique** (also part of metacognitive therapy, as described in Chapter 2) in which you practice shifting your attention away from worries and obsessive ruminations. It is easy to get caught in the pattern of focusing only on what you are thinking. This technique helps you to break this pattern and become focused on things outside of yourself.

See Dr. Wells's book (see references section for more information), record the 12-minute attention training script, and listen twice a day to learn how to shift your focus and attention away from OCD thoughts. The method involves looking at a dot (I use a red dot) on the wall and keeping your focus on the dot; you also focus on different sounds including a tapping noise, sounds that are occurring naturally around you, and other noises. You learn how to shift your attention between the different sounds. This training process allows you to become skilled at switching your attention away from your worries and obsessive thoughts in your mind and onto other things around you.

COMMON OCD THINKING PATTERNS AND BELIEFS

There are certain thinking patterns and beliefs that are commonly seen in people with OCD, and it is useful to identify which ones are relevant to you as this will help you to better understand what thoughts are coming from OCD. Many of these thinking patterns have to do with how you think about your thoughts and with what you think will happen if you think a certain way or think about certain things. If your parents or therapist want to know more about OCD thinking patterns, they can check out the books by Wilhelm and Steketee (2006) and Wells (2009), both of which are found in the References section of this book.

OVERESTIMATION OF DANGER

People with OCD tend to overestimate the risk of danger and have a core belief that the world is a threatening, dangerous place. As a result, they believe things need to be done to prevent harm and to keep oneself and one's loved ones safe. Included in this belief also is the idea that making mistakes and doing something wrong will lead to bad outcomes and responsibility for those outcomes. For example, Andrew thought it was easy to get sick from using public bathrooms, and so he labeled them as very dangerous and unsafe. He thought that if he didn't wash his hands thoroughly enough, he would be to blame for getting sick and for getting others sick as well. Sydney thought it was easy to step on an animal and kill it and thought walking outside was dangerous. Her worry about hurting or killing an animal was very strong.

DESIRE FOR CERTAINTY

Many children with OCD want to know *for sure* that something bad won't happen, or didn't happen, and end up doing a lot of doubting, checking, and asking behaviors in search of certainty. For example, Alicia wanted absolute certainty that her milk was safe and unspoiled, and even the expiration date wasn't good enough—she even doubted that it was correct.

PERFECTIONISM

This is the belief that things should be perfect, and that they aren't right or correct unless they are perfect. Not only does the child believe it is *possible* to be perfect, or to do things perfectly, but she is not comfortable and things don't feel right unless they are considered to be perfect. This belief often results in ordering, checking, redoing tasks, rewriting, and so on. For example, Jasmine couldn't relax when in her bed unless the blanket was perfectly flat, straight, and evenly distributed on the bed. She also had a hard time working at her desk unless everything was perfectly aligned.

RIGID/MORAL-THEMED THINKING

Some children with OCD, like William, have rigid thinking that is grounded in moral or religious ideals. This type of thinking assumes that there is a fundamental right and wrong and that a person can be punished by God or go to heaven or hell based on how he thinks or behaves. This usually results in a rigid way of behaving and living based on the fear of being punished or doomed. The person ends up doubting his own true self and that he is a good person at the core.

OVERIMPORTANCE OF THOUGHTS

In OCD, thoughts have a lot of meaning associated with them, and there often are faulty beliefs linked to the thoughts. Thoughts are considered to be as powerful as actions or events. This pattern of thinking magnifies the power of thoughts and makes it feel like thoughts are the same as actions or mean as much as actions do. Similarly, thoughts are considered to be true and accurate representations of what you really feel or want. In other words, there is no boundary between thinking about doing something and actually doing it.

Metacognitive therapy (MCT) calls these beliefs "fusion beliefs" and explains that **thought-event fusion** is when a person believes that a thought either causes an event to happen or means that it must have already happened. For example, Sydney believed that if she thought that she killed an animal, then that meant that it had actually happened (and she would go back and check to make sure). Another child had the thought of stabbing her baby brother, and she worried that it would happen (even though she didn't want or plan to do this) or that it already had happened (and this would cause her to check on her brother to make sure he was OK).

Thought-action fusion is when a person believes that having the thought or urge to do something will actually cause that person to do it. These thoughts can make the person feel out of control, and when thinking this way, she is not aware that she has 100% control over herself and her actions. When thinking this way, it feels like the thoughts have the control and can cause you to do something bad. For example, Kevin believed that if he had an intrusive thought about touching younger children in a sexual way, that he would actually do the inappropriate behavior! He believed that having the thought meant that he would act on it and that he was a pervert. Kevin had no desire to touch children inappropriately, and he was not a pervert; it was simply the thought he had, and that thought was a product of OCD.

These thoughts may sound really weird, but in fact, they are very common in OCD, and they don't mean that the person is going crazy or has lost touch with reality. These are just scary thoughts that feel very powerful, and this pattern ends up causing many children with OCD to be afraid of their thoughts. In Chapter 7, you will learn how to challenge these thoughts and make them less powerful by purposely saying them out loud, writing them down, and recording them. Through the exposure to the thoughts, and by preventing yourself from doing the ritual that usually follows (such as checking), you will disempower these thoughts and take control of OCD!

THINKING MISTAKES (ALSO CALLED "COGNITIVE DISTORTIONS")

Everyone makes thinking mistakes, or thinking errors, particularly when they are anxious. For example, some people are afraid to fly in an airplane, and either avoid flying or are very nervous when they fly. These people think flying is dangerous, and they worry that if they fly, they will die in a plane crash; this type of thinking is a thinking error called "catastrophizing." It is a thinking error because flying is not dangerous. That conclusion is based on fear, not on reality. In fact, flying is the safest form of transportation and very safe in general. Although planes do crash, the large majority of the time, they do not. In fact, one's chances of dying in a plane crash are 1 in 4.6 million. This is a very, very low risk, and one's chances of winning the lottery are actually better! Therefore, being on a plane often is the *safest* place to be! Catastrophizing is when someone uses "what if . . ." thinking, ends up thinking about the worst-case scenario, and often acts as if the disaster will happen. When working to overcome anxiety, a person needs to identify and replace her thinking errors.

TYPES OF THINKING ERRORS

1. *Catastrophizing*: Visualizing disaster, thinking that the worst thing is going to happen and feeling like you wouldn't be able to handle it; asking "What if . . .?"
    - ☞ Example: What if the cookies were cooked with bad eggs and I get salmonella poisoning?
    - ☞ Example: What if I touch the toilet seat and get AIDS?

2. *All-or-Nothing*: Thinking in extremes, meaning that things are either perfect or a failure; there is no middle ground—it's either one extreme or another; thinking in an inflexible way.
    - ☞ Example: My shoes have to be completely organized in my closet, or else my whole closet is not neat and not organized.
    - ☞ Example: Going out on a school night is wrong. I will only let myself go out on weekends.

3. *Superstitious Thinking*: Thinking that by doing something, you will cause or prevent something else from happening.
    - ☞ Example: "If I tell my parents I love them three times before bed, we will all be safe. If I don't say goodnight in the right order, something bad might happen."
    - ☞ Example: "If I knock on wood whenever I have a bad thought, then nothing bad will happen to me."

4. *Magical Thinking*: Thinking some things are lucky and some things are unlucky, such as numbers.
   - ☞ Example: "The number four is lucky, so I will buy the fourth magazine, use the fourth tissue, and knock on wood four times."
   - ☞ Example: "There are good signs and bad signs. If I hear a certain song, I know that it's a bad sign and something bad will happen, so I should turn off the radio."

5. *Selective Attention*: Paying attention to information that confirms your beliefs; ignoring evidence that goes against what you believe.
   - ☞ Example: Food can be dangerous and cause you to die. Several foods were on recall last year, and many people got salmonella and other diseases from eating contaminated meat.
   - ☞ Example: Bathrooms are dirty places, especially doorknobs. I remember that one time a man used the toilet and then didn't wash his hands and touched the doorknob.

6. *Magnifying*: Making something seem bigger and worse than it really is; turning up the volume on anything bad, making it worse.
   - ☞ Example: You have a cough and feel sick and start to think about missing school and the work you will miss and how it will be impossible to catch up.
   - ☞ Example: When your dad parallel-parked the car, he lightly bumped the car behind him and you got very upset, called it an accident, and wanted to leave a note.

7. *Shoulds*: Having rules about how things should be; using the words "should," "must," and "ought to" to show how things should be.
   - ☞ Example: You make a mistake and forget to hand in an assignment. When you hand it in the next day, your teacher marks it down to a "B" because it is late. You feel so upset with yourself and think, "I shouldn't make mistakes like this. That was so stupid of me."
   - ☞ Example: I shouldn't upset or disappoint my friends. Others should think only good things about me.

8. *Probability Overestimation*: Overestimating the likelihood that something bad will happen.
   - ☞ Example: I will get sick if I eat yogurt that expired yesterday.
   - ☞ Example: Sitting near a sick kid will guarantee I will catch his cold.

If you or your parents want to read more about thinking errors, check out the books by Burns (1999), Hyman and Pedrick (2005), and Antony and Swinson (2008), all listed in the References section of this book.

REPLACING YOUR ANXIOUS THOUGHTS

Once you have identified which thinking errors you make, the next step is to practice challenging them and replacing them with more realistic thoughts. The goal is to come up with balanced, neutral thoughts, rather than positive ones. For example, instead of thinking that you will get sick from eating yogurt that expired yesterday, you can think that most likely you will not get sick and that the expiration date is not an exact calculation. You also can think that many people eat yogurt that expired yesterday without getting sick. For example, instead of thinking that going out on school nights is wrong, you might challenge that idea and ask yourself, "What is really wrong about it? What would I do instead of going out? Is going out any different than watching TV at home?" For example, instead of thinking that you can't do work unless everything on your desk is aligned and in order, try reading one paragraph of your book while things are out of order, just to see if you are capable of reading while things are not perfect on your desk.

To replace your thoughts, you want to "consider the facts" and ask yourself, "What proof do I have that this thought is correct?" For example, what proof do you have that you will get AIDS from using a public bathroom? What proof do you have that going out on a weekday is bad or wrong, or that it will lead to punishment? What proof do you have that eating cookies is dangerous?

Although I discourage searching the Internet for answers (usually because someone with OCD or anxiety will use selective attention to find information that confirms his or her anxious beliefs), it can be useful, particularly if your parents assist you, to do an information-gathering search from respectable and reputable sites to get the facts. For example, Andrew and I did an Internet search on methods of getting HIV/AIDS because during his treatment, he shared that he was afraid that he could get AIDS from using a public bathroom. We looked on sites that ended in .gov and also referred to the Whitman-Walker website and found useful information on how someone can contract AIDS (and by the way, you *cannot* get AIDS from using a public bathroom). Gathering the facts was helpful for Andrew, and he used the information to challenge his catastrophic fears and OCD thoughts.

Challenge your anxious thoughts by asking yourself, "What would someone without OCD think in this situation?" or "What would someone who is not anxious in this situation think right now?" Consider what a positive outcome might look like. I can tell you countless examples of situations in which the worst-case scenario could have happened, and it didn't. For example, one day I came home to find that the gas stove in my kitchen was completely on, and it had been on for several hours while no one was home! Someone had mistakenly left it on, and the flame had been on for hours, with no bad outcome. There was no fire, no danger, and nothing was wrong. I also know of many people who have left candles burning in their homes by mistake, and nothing bad happened. Dr. Mary Alvord, a psychologist with whom I work, told me that years ago, she and her family went on vacation for 2 weeks and someone forgot to lock their front door. So here they were, out of the state for 2 weeks with the front door of their house left unlocked, and nothing happened—no burglars broke in and no one stole anything! Their house was totally fine. These stories are good reminders that even when there is potential for a problem, it doesn't mean that a problem will occur. Much of the time, things work out just fine.

Another useful strategy to challenge your thinking errors is to write down your thoughts in a journal. You can make three columns: one for your automatic thought, one to label the thinking error you used, and one to write a new, balanced thought to re-place it.

SELF-TALK: TALKING BACK TO THE OCD

Self-talk is what you say to yourself. When you are feeling anxious or triggered by OCD, your self-talk is negative. An example of negative self-talk is, "I can't handle this. It's bet-ter to keep washing my hands until the OCD feels OK."

self-talk: what you say to yourself; when you are feeling anxious or triggered by OCD, your self-talk is negative

One goal in challenging your thoughts is to change your self-talk, making it more positive and empowering. Here are examples of positive self-talk:

> ➤ "I can handle this."
> ➤ "I can change the way I think to change the way I feel."
> ➤ "I must face my fears to overcome them. I can do it."
> ➤ "I am uncomfortable, but I am fine."
> ➤ "I am scared, but I am safe."
> ➤ "I can help myself relax. Let me do my calm breathing."
> ➤ "It is just the OCD talking. Someone without OCD wouldn't be having this thought. I don't have to listen to the OCD."
> ➤ "Everything is OK. It will all work out."

Left unchallenged, the OCD will continue to gain power and strength. By continually challenging your OCD, changing what you say to yourself, and replacing your thoughts, you will gain power and strength and *take control of OCD*!

What I Know Now

This chapter focused on the thoughts part of OCD. You learned about identifying your OCD thoughts and completed the section called "When my OCD talks, it says . . . ." You examined ways to master your worries, including making a worry tape and using detached mindfulness. Common OCD thinking patterns were reviewed, and you learned how to replace your anxious thoughts. Finally, self-talk was discussed and you learned how to have positive self-talk and talk back to your OCD.

CHAPTER 6
TOLERATING UNCERTAINTY

"The hardest part of having OCD is that the worry doesn't end. I worry about how something may have happened that will cause me to be sick years from now. It's about the uncertainty of what will happen; maybe I won't know that I got contaminated with some illness that won't come out until much later."

—**Frank, age 13**

One of the main difficulties faced by children with OCD is being able to tolerate uncertainty. Uncertainty means not knowing for sure. Tolerating something means being able to handle it. So, being able to *tolerate uncertainty* means being able to handle not knowing for sure.

When you have OCD, it makes you feel like you need to know for absolute sure that something did or didn't happen, or that something could or could not happen. OCD causes you to keep repeating the thoughts of

tolerating uncertainty: being able to handle not knowing for sure

"What if . . ." and worrying about what might have happened. This desire for certainty is at the root of many of your OCD worries, thoughts, and behaviors. This chapter is about challenging those thoughts and learning how to be OK with not knowing. Therefore, this chapter also is about the thoughts part of OCD.

OCD AND UNCERTAINTY

As you work toward taking control of OCD, you are figuring out how OCD influences your thinking and twists the way that you see things. You are starting to see how OCD works and how it makes you think. For example, OCD makes you focus on potential threats; it keeps your attention focused on what could go wrong. OCD also gets stronger and more powerful when there is uncertainty, or ambiguity, in a situation. When something is ambiguous, it is unclear, vague, or uncertain. If there is any room for doubt, OCD will try to gain power from it. As discussed in Chapter 5, this desire for certainty is a type of OCD thinking pattern.

For example, when Sydney stepped on something without seeing what it was, the OCD would make her worry that it was animal that she stepped on. Because she didn't see what she stepped on, there was some uncertainty in the situation. Even though she would have known if she had stepped on an animal, the OCD made her think that she could've stepped on an animal without knowing it. The OCD made her doubt what happened.

This idea of not knowing what you did, or what you saw, is a big theme in OCD. I have worked with many children who have worried that they did something, such as leave the oven on, leave the door open or unlocked, or hurt someone, and many of them worry that they did these things without knowing it or without remembering it. In this way, OCD can make you feel crazy and like you don't know what happened in reality. It is very important that you recognize that this type of thinking and this type of experience are only *symptoms* of OCD.

DOUBTS: WHERE CHECKING BEHAVIOR COMES FROM

Checking is a common OCD behavior (ritual), usually done to decrease the anxiety that comes from an upsetting thought about something bad happening. Therefore, checking comes from doubts about what might have occurred. When there is any amount of uncertainty, OCD makes you doubt. Because Sydney had doubts about what she stepped on, she retraced her steps to make sure she hadn't hurt any animals. Alicia had doubts about the safety of the food she ate, so she would check the expiration dates again, or would ask her mom to tell her she was safe. Asking her mom was another form of checking behavior ("I am checking with Mom to make sure the food was safe"). Sometimes Kevin would get so worried and anxious that he might have hurt a younger child without knowing it that he would check the newspaper to make sure there were no reports that he had done so!

The motivation for these checking behaviors is to try to know something for sure; the motivation is certainty. The problem is that OCD makes you feel like you could *never* be certain. Even when you check and try to know something for sure, OCD will not be satisfied—OCD will still make you have doubts and want you to keep checking, over and over again.

UNCERTAINTY AS A PART OF LIFE

As much as we would like to know how things will turn out, this is not how life goes. And, to be honest with you, life would not be that enjoyable or exciting if we were able to know how things will turn out. Part of the joy of life is watching it unfold and experiencing things that come along in your life when they naturally come along. Part of overcoming OCD is talking back to it and telling it that you won't try to gain certainty, not only because you don't want to be ruled by OCD, but because gaining certainty is not possible.

As you grow up, one life goal is to work toward accepting that uncertainty is a part of life, and to try your hardest (using the strategies described in this book) to enjoy life without worrying so much about it. You can use mindfulness and practice being in the present moment to help you reach the goal of accepting uncertainty.

When you worry, you associate not knowing with danger; however, not knowing is actually neither good nor bad—it is just neutral. This is similar to when you challenge thinking errors by replacing the negative thoughts with neutral ones. It's the same concept: When you don't know something for sure, try to make it something neutral, rather than something bad. So, you might say to yourself, "Not knowing for sure is neither good nor bad. It is in between. The outcome can be good or bad, but at this moment in time, it is simply neutral."

UNCERTAINTY TRAINING EXERCISE

Dr. Robert Leahy, a psychologist in New York City and author of the 2006 book *The Worry Cure*, explained that uncertainty training will help you be better able to tolerate not knowing. Uncertainty training involves saying your fear repeatedly for a practice period every day. For example, you say: "It is always possible that (add your fear here)" for 10–20 minutes every day. Eventually, you can tolerate the uncertainty of what could happen. When doing this, you want to make sure you are alert and paying attention to what you are saying; also, you want to try to feel the emotions that usually come with hearing this scary thought. It is important that you try not to *neutralize* the thought, or make it seem less scary. So, you would *not* want to say, "It is always possible that I left the stove on, but most likely I turned it off"; that last part—"but most likely I turned it off"—is a neutralizer, and when you add this, you don't get the benefit of really getting used to your fear. Therefore, when you practice, you want to keep your statements to just the worries (do not add ideas that would make you feel better).

uncertainty training: saying your fear repeatedly for a practice period every day; eventually, you become used to tolerating the uncertainty of what could happen

For example, Andrew said: "It is always possible that I have germs on my hands from using the bathroom," and "It is always possible that I will get sick." Alicia's statement was: "It is always possible that the milk was expired and I will throw up." Sydney's uncertainty training statement was: "It is always possible that I killed an animal." William said: "It is always possible that I will be punished for having fun and feeling pleasure." Even though these thoughts were very unlikely (if not impossible, for example, in William's case), each person struggled with these thoughts and ideas that these bad outcomes could happen. Their OCD made them believe that the idea was not only possible, but very likely.

By practicing uncertainty training, each of these children learned how to handle having these bad thoughts and not acting on them. By practicing having the thought many times, and feeling the emotions that accompany these scary thoughts, you will learn to "desensitize," or become used to or numb to, the thought. In fact, the thought will no longer be alarming to you. You will learn how to be able to handle the idea of not knowing for sure, and you will be one more step closer to taking control of OCD!

For the next few weeks, try the uncertainty training exercise. Set aside 10 minutes twice a day (or one 15-minute time period) to do uncertainty training. You can do this instead of worry time or as part of worry time.

➤ Complete the sentence: "It is always possible that _____," by filling in your OCD fear(s).

➤ You can do several different sentences like this one, all beginning with "It is always possible that _____" (with different endings), but the worries should be related. For example, "It is always possible that the milk was old. It is always possible that I will get sick. It is always possible that I will throw up."

➤ Practice saying the statements, and really try to have the anxious feelings that thinking these thoughts usually brings up as you do this. Keep practicing until you are able to have these thoughts without feeling anxious; practice until they no longer seem alarming to you!

UNCERTAINTY TRAINING VS. SELF-TALK

It is important to make clear the difference between uncertainty training and self-talk, because it's easy to be confused by what I am encouraging you to do using these two opposite techniques. Self-talk involves telling yourself that it will be OK, that you are scared but safe, etc. Uncertainty training focuses on being able to handle the idea of not being safe or having things not work out well. These two can, and should, be used to take control of OCD, but the difference is *when* you use each:

➤ **Self-talk** is good to use when you are actually doing the exposures and facing your fears. It helps you manage the challenge of facing your fears and prevents your rituals. It helps you to be stronger and gain more confidence in taking control of OCD.

➤ **Uncertainty training**, on the other hand, is *not* to be used when doing the exposures or facing your fears. Instead, uncertainty training is a separate practice that you do at a different time, preferably a time when you are not very anxious or worried. The uncertainty training helps you be better able to manage doubts and not knowing for sure, but it is designed to be used at a specific time, *not* when you are facing your fears. The benefits of uncertainty training, however, will ultimately help you manage the exposures better.

What I Know Now

This chapter focused on helping you learn how to be able to handle uncertainty and discussed the connection between OCD and a desire for certainty. The connection between doubts and checking behavior also was explained. You learned that uncertainty is a part of life, and that being able to accept this is part of growing up. Finally, you read about how to do uncertainty training and how to practice the technique.

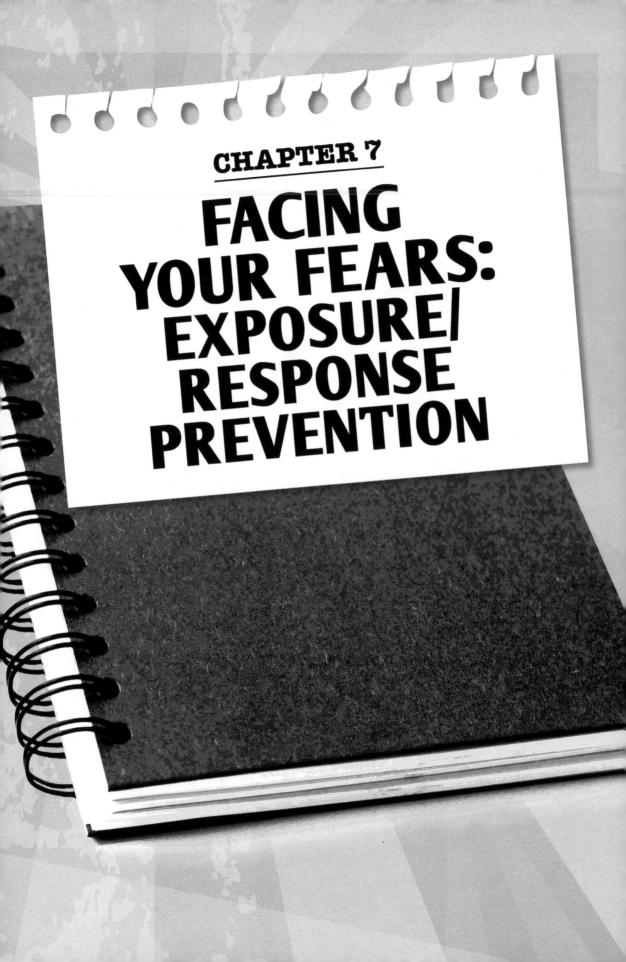

CHAPTER 7

FACING YOUR FEARS: EXPOSURE/ RESPONSE PREVENTION

> "Even though it's hard to deal with, eventually you get through it. If you work toward it and concentrate, in the end it's worth it—it gets easier."
>
> —**Sophie, age 12**

Congratulations on getting to this chapter! Up until now, all of the chapters have been focused on helping you get to this point. By learning about OCD and preparing for the phase of challenging your OCD behaviors, you are now ready to start facing your fears! This chapter and the next one are about doing exposures, which address the *behavior* part of OCD. Before we get into it, let's review everything you have learned up until this point:

- ➤ Definition of OCD
- ➤ Common types of obsessions and compulsions
- ➤ The OCD cycle
- ➤ Cognitive-behavioral therapy (CBT; the most effective treatment for OCD)
- ➤ The three parts of OCD/anxiety: body, thoughts, and behavior
- ➤ Exposure/response prevention (E/RP)
- ➤ Metacognitive therapy (MCT; including attention training technique and detached mindfulness)
- ➤ Mindfulness
- ➤ Medication
- ➤ Being proactive and hopeful and asking for support
- ➤ The importance of making a ladder and how to make your own
- ➤ Sample ladders of children with OCD
- ➤ Relaxation techniques
  - ☛ calm breathing (lower diaphragmatic breathing and one-nostril breathing)
  - ☛ progressive muscle relaxation (PMR)
  - ☛ relaxing imagery
  - ☛ mindfulness meditation
  - ☛ yoga (standing mountain, downward-facing dog, and child's pose)

➤ How to identify your OCD thoughts ("When my OCD talks, it says . . .")

➤ How to master your worries (for example, reframing your worries, making a worry tape)

➤ Common OCD beliefs (such as overrating danger, desire for certainty, and fusion beliefs)

➤ Thinking mistakes (for example, catastrophizing, superstitious thinking, shoulds)

➤ How to replace your anxious thoughts

➤ Self-talk

➤ Uncertainty training

If any part of the above list seems unfamiliar, or like you may have forgotten it, then it is a good idea to go back and review the sections in the previous chapters, as all of the above information is useful and important for facing your fears.

EXPOSURE/RESPONSE PREVENTION (E/RP)

In Chapter 2, you learned about the idea of "exposure" to your feared situations and that "exposure/response prevention" (E/RP) is the best way to overcome OCD. As explained before, E/RP involves facing your fears, one by one, and preventing yourself from doing the ritual or behavior that you usually do in response to that situation. For example, Andrew would sit next to someone who was sick (exposure) without washing his hands afterward (response prevention); Alicia would eat food from bake sales and sample trays in grocery stores (exposures) without asking questions afterward such as asking the people at the bake sale about their cooking methods and asking her mom to assure her that she would not get sick (response preventions); Jasmine would mismatch her socks in her closet (exposure) without rearranging them to make them "correct" (response prevention), and she would turn things around in her room (exposure) without adjusting them back to their "correct" positions (response prevention); and Kevin would walk by parks with children playing to purposefully have the OCD thoughts about hurting them (exposure), without shaking his head (response prevention). When you do E/RP, you challenge the OCD and train yourself to respond appropriately, as someone without OCD would.

When Andrew, Alicia, Jasmine, and Kevin did their exposures, their anxiety levels increased: they felt anxious and had anxious thoughts. Without doing their usual "neutralizing rituals" or behaviors that they would do to decrease their anxiety, they would feel more of the anxiety. Each of these children had to remind themselves that it would get worse before it got better and that they would have anxiety in the short-term (when doing E/RP) in order to be anxiety-free in the long-term. They had to remember that while their usual rituals and behaviors helped them to feel relief in the moment, those rituals and behaviors actually strengthened their OCD and kept OCD around in the future. Andrew, Alicia, Jasmine, and Kevin also used all of the strategies they learned to be able to cope with the exposures; for example, they used relaxation, positive self-talk, and replacement thoughts to be better able to handle the exposures.

WHY EXPOSURE WORKS

The theory behind exposure is that once you stay in a scary or uncomfortable situation long enough, and practice it enough times, you will get used to it, and it will no longer cause you to feel anxious. This process is called "habituation," which means that you will habituate to, or get used to, the situation.

The best way to understand habituation is to think about a freezing cold swimming pool. If you were to jump in and then jump out immediately, you would conclude that pools

habituation: once you stay in a scary or uncomfortable situation long enough, and practice it enough times, you will get used to it and it will no longer cause you to feel anxious

are unpleasant and uncomfortable. If you continued to do this (quickly jumping in and out) each time you saw a freezing cold swimming pool, all you would do is strengthen this belief that pools are uncomfortable and that you don't like them. However, if you got in the pool and made yourself stay there, you would gradually become more relaxed and more comfortable, and you would learn that pools are not that bad after all. After 5 minutes, you would start to breathe easier, then after 10 minutes, you would be able to go further in, and after 15 minutes, you would no longer feel freezing. In fact, the water would start to feel warmer to you—even though the water temperature itself didn't really change (for example, anyone new to come in to the pool would consider it freezing)—because you have become used to it. The longer you stayed in it, the more comfortable you would feel. It's the same thing with anxiety and OCD: Once you stay in an anxiety-provoking situation for long enough, it will no longer cause you to feel anxiety. Your anxiety will decrease, and the situation itself will become more neutral to you.

When you do the exposures and take the steps on your ladder, you will see the process of habituation happen. You will see yourself becoming more comfortable in situations you have typically avoided in the past.

When you challenge your OCD purposefully by doing the exposures on your ladder, you shift the power so that OCD has less power and you have more. This change in the power dynamic allows you to take control of OCD. By being in your trigger situations without doing the behaviors you usually do (such as repetitive checking), you have the chance to learn that your beliefs about bad things happening are untrue. You also have become one step closer to not being organized or influenced by OCD, because you will be able to prevent yourself from doing the OCD behaviors.

THREE KEYS TO DOING EXPOSURES

When doing exposures, you want to keep in mind the three keys to exposure:

1. repetitive
2. frequent
3. prolonged

You want to do each step on your ladder *repetitively*, meaning that you do that step over and over again until it no longer causes you anxiety. Once you have practiced a step enough times for it to not cause you anxiety, then it should be part of your normal behavior. Therefore, you repeat each step many times until it no longer belongs on your ladder!

You want to do the exposure to the step *frequently*, meaning that you practice taking the step as often as possible. When you do something frequently, you do it a lot. So, in addition to practicing the same step over and over (compared to just doing it once), you practice that step often and many times (frequently). Ideally, you should plan to do practices from your ladder almost every day (because most kids with OCD do their OCD behaviors every day).

You want to stay in the exposure for a *prolonged* period of time, long enough to see your anxiety level decrease. Prolonged means for a long, extended period of time. If you only stay in the situation for a short time, it will be harder to get used to it. Also, if you do this, you may reinforce, or strengthen, your negative feelings about the situation; because you didn't stay in it long enough to reach the point of calming down, then you will only remember that you felt anxious. Think about the swimming pool again: If you didn't like pools in the first place, and then quickly jumped in and out, all you would do would be to reinforce or strengthen your belief that swimming

> **prolonged:** for a long, extended period of time; you want to stay in the exposure long enough to see your anxiety level decrease

pools are uncomfortable. You would only remember how freezing cold it was and how cold you were, and you would not have had the chance to get used to it and realize that it would feel warm in about 15 minutes!

So, when you do the steps on your ladder, make sure to **repeat** each step, do it **frequently**, and stay in it for a **prolonged** period of time!

USING YOUR LADDER AND PLANNING YOUR EXPOSURES

In Chapter 3, you developed your ladder and ranked the situations that make you anxious that you tend to avoid. Now is the time to refer to your ladder and plan your first exposure.

Your ladder will guide you on what steps to take and the order in which you should take them. As a general rule, you should take one step at a time and not move ahead to the next step until you have habituated to the step below it. Again, you may realize along the way that the order you put your steps in might need to be changed. It also is very important to remember that you can break steps down into smaller steps. The main goal is to be working on your exposures, even if you are breaking them down into very small steps.

Start with making a plan to take the first step on the ladder, including which coping strategies you will use. The more detailed your plan, the better. For example, Jasmine's first step was to leave her backpack zipper partially opened. She developed the following plan to take the step, including which strategies would help:

Unzip my backpack and then when zipping it back up, leave a gap of about 2 inches. Immediately take a step back from the backpack (so it's not within my arm's reach) and do calm breathing to stay as relaxed as possible. While looking at the zipper and noticing how it's not zipped correctly, use self-talk to remind myself that I need to stay with the feelings of discomfort and that I will feel better soon. Also, remind myself that this wouldn't bother most people and it's only bothering me because of OCD. I can't listen to the OCD anymore. I will get to the point where I realize

*that it doesn't matter that the zipper is not fully closed and that
I can feel OK even when I don't fix it.*

Thinking about how she will handle her feelings of discomfort, and identifying specific strategies that she will use (calm breathing, self-talk), Jasmine was able to be successful during the exposure and prevent her usual response of zipping the backpack completely.

Jasmine continued to make detailed plans for the first several steps. For example, her third step was to pack an odd number of underwear, shorts, and T-shirts for sleep-away camp. She developed the following plan to take the step, including which strategies would help:

> *Plan to pack on Sunday and have Mom help me with what to bring. Because I am packing for 2 weeks, and will get to wash my clothes, I will pack nine pairs of underwear, five pairs of shorts, and seven T-shirts. As soon as I've picked out the clothes, I will have Mom put them in the duffle bag and move the duffle bag to the garage. This way, I won't be tempted to add anything to it. I will use calm breathing if I notice my body feeling tense, and self-talk to remind myself that I can handle this and that it will be OK. I also will remind myself that I am practicing being able to let things be, even though it doesn't feel right to me. I believe that if I stick with it, the urge to add more clothes to make an even number will go away. If I continue to focus on it, I will try distraction by repeating the ABCs and making lists; or I will use detached mindfulness to separate myself from my thoughts and try to become an observer to my thoughts, rather than reacting to them.*

After developing plans for the first several steps, Jasmine got the hang of it and didn't need to do as much preparation for the rest of the steps. Throughout the exposure period, however, she continued to review her self-talk statements and kept a journal of her thoughts, labeling her thinking errors and OCD beliefs as they came up.

Similarly, William made detailed plans for many of the steps on his ladder, which included the strategies he would use to cope with anxiety during the exposures. His first step was to not do homework on weekend nights. He ranked this step the easiest because there had been weekend nights in the past when he did not do homework and felt fine; however, these were the exception to the rule, as he usually did homework on Friday and Saturday evenings.

William planned to rent a movie on Friday night and planned to go out with his friends on Saturday night. We discussed that going out with his friends was going to be harder, because it was more fun, and he felt guilty when he was having fun and enjoying himself. He planned to watch the movie in the basement, away from his desk and homework, and to use self-talk to deal with any anxiety or discomfort that came up. He made the following self-talk note cards for this situation: "It is perfectly reasonable to watch a movie and relax on a weekend night. I have worked hard all week and need this down-time to be a healthy person. Even if it doesn't feel right to do this, I know it's a very normal and acceptable thing to do. The bad feeling is only my OCD and I won't listen to it. I will fight the OCD and the urge to do homework and try to keep my focus on the movie. I am on top of my work, and the only reason I would do work tonight is because of OCD, nothing else."

For Saturday night, William asked his closest friend Mike to go out for pizza and to see a movie. If at any point William felt anxiety, he planned on using mindfulness and calm breathing. He had practiced mindfulness and being attuned to the present moment and planned to use those skills to deal with the situation. He knew that in focusing on the present moment, he would direct his attention to what he was doing, reminding himself that the present was the only moment that was important. Any thoughts about homework were a signal to him that he was not in the present moment, and he would direct his attention back to what he was doing—eating pizza, talking to Mike, or watching the movie. He also planned to use the same self-talk statements that he used for the Friday night exposure. William expected Saturday night to be more challenging for two reasons: He would not have done homework on Friday *and* he was out with a friend, which meant he was having fun and doing something pleasurable. Therefore, William also planned on doing calm breathing and progressive muscle relaxation during the movie if he felt tense. He also promised himself that he wouldn't disappoint Mike by cancelling and asked his parents to give him extra encouragement to stick with the plan.

Both Jasmine and William benefitted from having a detailed plan of how they would cope with their exposures and any anxiety that they felt in the process. Having a plan made both of them feel more confident and organized about doing the exposures, and they felt like they had a clear idea of what to do with the anxiety when it came up.

Creating a detailed plan also will help you in doing your exposures. When developing your own plan, try to be as specific as possible and also plan for any obstacles that may get in the way of doing your exposure. An example of an obstacle may be having thought "It's not a big deal to just . . . (straighten your desk, put one thing away, not eat this cookie, do a little homework on Saturday night before I go out)." When OCD minimizes the behavior, it seems easier to do it than not to do it; this is a potential obstacle, and you want to plan for how you will deal with that thought. For example, you might talk back to the OCD and say, "That's right—it's not a big deal either way. Doing homework or not doing homework before I go out won't make a difference in the big picture of school or my grades; however, it will make a big difference in overcoming OCD." Therefore, another key part of doing the exposures is challenging your OCD thoughts and beliefs as they come up.

Remember that it's the OCD thoughts and beliefs that usually make kids do the compulsive behaviors like checking, asking, or redoing, and it's these thoughts that cause kids to avoid certain situations. So, when making a plan for each exposure, make sure to include what you will do to challenge your OCD thoughts and beliefs—what will you say in talking back to the OCD? What will your replacement thoughts be like? How will you challenge your OCD beliefs? For example, the *desire for certainty* belief can be challenged by saying back, "I don't need to be certain and don't need to know for sure. There are plenty of times I don't know for sure, and the outcome is fine. Tolerating uncertainty is not only a part of overcoming OCD, but it's a part of life!"

When you have a thinking error, label it as a thinking error and come up with a replacement thought; for example, when Alicia had the thought about getting salmonella poisoning and throwing up, she would tell herself,

> *That is catastrophizing, my favorite thinking error! I won't let thinking errors make the OCD stronger. I can reassure myself that the risk of getting salmonella is very low, but I can also deal with the uncertainty and the possibility that I could get it. I could handle whatever happens. Let me think about what someone without OCD would do in this situation. Probably they would eat the cookies and focus on how good they taste.*

If Alicia does this each time she makes a catastrophizing thinking error, she will eventually stop making them. However, if she doesn't challenge the thought, and instead does the checking and asking behavior, she will continue to make these thinking mistakes, and her OCD will become stronger.

If you find yourself catastrophizing, replace your thoughts with factual information, come up with a neutral way of thinking about the situation, or use it as an opportunity to practice tolerating uncertainty. If you find yourself organized by shoulds, label the shoulds and come up with a replacement thought such as, "It is OK to make mistakes—it makes me human. I will disappoint others, and they will disappoint me; I am still going to have great friends, even though we will all sometimes upset one another." If you find yourself having fusion beliefs, label them as fusion beliefs and replace the though. For example, say

> *A thought is just a thought. A thought is not the same as an action. I can have any thought I'd like, and it doesn't mean it will happen. I could think to myself, "I have a million dollars" and it won't mean anything—it doesn't mean that I have a million dollars or will have a million dollars. If it did, then everyone would be a millionaire!*

Remember that when you have OCD, you get stuck in a pattern of thinking too much and overthinking situations. It is easy to get locked in a way of thinking, and thinking, and thinking. Many kids even start to think about their thinking itself! It may be useful to keep in mind the saying, "Don't overthink it!" and simplify what you are doing, much like an observer of your behavior would do. For example, instead of thinking about each move you are making in the bathroom and what you might be touching and how you might be touching it and where the germs are and what might happen if you get germs on you (a classic pattern of OCD thinking), you could reframe it by saying, "It's just going to the bathroom." Anyone watching you would say, "He's just going to the bathroom." They certainly would *not* say, "He's getting contaminated with some terminal disease!" (because this is not possible, or else everyone would have diseases because everyone uses bathrooms). By doing this, you are simplifying your thought process, interrupting the OCD train of thought, and using rational self-talk to reduce your anxiety.

Again, by challenging your thoughts all of the time, when they come up (especially during the exposures), you will break the pattern of thinking this way. You will cause a shift in how you automatically think, and when you pair this with doing Exposure/Response Prevention and facing your fears, you will take control of OCD and return to living anxiety-free!

In the space below, or on a separate sheet of paper, write down your plan for the first step on your ladder. Make the plan about what you will do and exactly how you will do it. Try to be as detailed as possible and include all the ways you can calm your body and challenge your thoughts. Refer to Jasmine and William's plans above for examples.

My Plan . . .

A NOTE ABOUT HOARDING AND EXPOSURES

In Chapter 1, hoarding was listed as a type of compulsion. Hoarding is when someone collects and saves an enormous amount of stuff and refuses to get rid of it. The amount of stuff is usually so large that it causes a problem for the person. Hoarding is more than just hav-

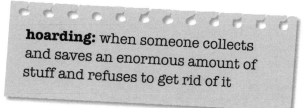

hoarding: when someone collects and saves an enormous amount of stuff and refuses to get rid of it

ing a messy room or finding it hard to get rid of things like toys or old books. Rather, hoarding is a more serious problem in which the person's possessions get in the way of normal activity, such as when a room is so full of stuff that it can't be used for other purposes or there is so much in one space that it is a fire hazard.

Exposures for hoarding typically require assistance from others. Most of the time, the person who hoards cannot get rid of her things on her own, and she needs someone else to help her through the process. Someone who is hoarding needs to learn how to sort through her belongings, make decisions regarding what to keep and what to throw out, and learn how to challenge her thoughts around the hoarding behavior. By taking small step exposures, such as not bringing any additional things into the home, and gradually getting rid of some of the piles, the person learns that she can handle the process of cleaning out.

TOLERATING ANXIETY DURING EXPOSURES

When doing your exposures, it is important that you also are exposing yourself to the feelings of anxiety itself. The goal is to tolerate the anxiety that naturally comes up, rather than trying to distract yourself from it. When you handle the feelings that arise from the exposures, you improve your ability to handle strong emotions like anxiety in general. Doing this allows you to become less influenced by the anxiety in the big picture.

Alicia had a hard time tolerating anxiety during the exposures at first. When she would eat foods as part of her exposure (for example, food from a bake sale or trigger foods like grilled cheese and tomatoes), she would watch television to distract herself and be able to "get through" the exposure. Although this "getting through it" approach technically allowed her to check off steps from her ladder, it didn't allow her to really habituate to them. Alicia distracted herself from the experience of facing her fears and doing the steps on her ladder, so she missed the goal of being able to tolerate the anxiety and discomfort. When I was working with Alicia, we discussed her tendency to focus on TV to deal with the exposures and discussed how she could use mindfulness to stay present in the situation. She then repeated the steps on her ladder without watching TV, and although it was difficult at times, she learned that she could handle the anxiety, and as she did, it would decrease.

Ways to tolerate anxiety during the exposures include: mindfulness, calm breathing, and self-talk. For example, when the anxiety comes up, you can recognize it and note that it is there, do calm breathing, and remind yourself that you can handle it and that feeling anxious is not a sign that anything bad will happen. Also, remind yourself that you can handle anything that comes your way. With practice, you will start to change your experience of anxiety, see it for what it is, and not react to it.

MOTIVATING YOURSELF

The exposure phase is the most important part of overcoming OCD. It is when you apply all of the information that you have learned about OCD, as well as the coping strategies, and decide to take control of OCD. Yet it also is the most challenging part and the one that requires you to be the strongest, most determined, and most confident. You have made a decision to fight your OCD and not let it control your life anymore. Whenever you feel discouraged, try to remember this mindset and also ask for help from parents if you need it. It is completely normal to find the exposures challenging but I am 100% certain that if you stick with it and continue to do them, it will get easier and you will feel better.

Remind yourself of the concepts discussed at the end of Chapter 2, including being proactive, being hopeful, and believing in yourself. Use the strategies reviewed above, particularly calm breathing, positive self-talk, replacing thinking errors with balanced thoughts, and using mindfulness, to cope with the exposures.

It is very helpful to reward yourself each time you do an exposure by marking the step on your calendar with either a star sticker or a check. Seeing your progress visually—as stickers or checks add up—allows you to feel more energized and excited about the great work you are doing. It also highlights how far you are getting in facing your fears and taking control of OCD. This usually makes kids more motivated to move up their ladders!

Finally, here is one more thing to keep in mind, which is very important: **behavior change happens first; cognitive change happens second**. This means that you will be able to change your behavior and take the steps on your ladder *before* you will stop having the OCD thoughts and urges to do the rituals such as checking. With time, changing your behavior and not doing your typical OCD behaviors and rituals will lead to changes in your thoughts (cognitive changes). Eventually the OCD thoughts will stop.

> **Remember:**
> **Behavior change happens first; cognitive change happens second.**

TAKING THE FIRST STEP

Now that you have finished reading the first seven chapters, it is time to take the first step on your ladder (use the plan you developed earlier). After you have done the first step enough times to be able to do it without feeling anxious, move up to the next step. Continue this process and work toward facing all of the steps on your ladder. The next chapter also is about facing your fears.

What I Know Now

This chapter focused on preparing you to face your fears. The process of exposure/response prevention (E/RP) was described in detail, and the theory behind exposure was explained. You learned about habituation and how you can habituate to, or become used to, your OCD situations as you practice them repetitively and frequently and stay in them for a prolonged period of time. You learned how to use your ladder and make detailed plans for your steps including which strategies you will use to cope with the exposures. The importance of tolerating anxiety and not distracting yourself was discussed. Finally, you read about how to motivate yourself throughout the process.

CHAPTER 8

BECOMING RESILIENT TO OCD:

Going the Extra Mile With Exposures

"When facing my fears, I used a lot of self-talk. I read my note cards twice a day and ended up memorizing them. I would tell myself that there was only one way to get rid of this OCD and that was to face my fears. When I got to the top and finished my ladder, I realized how much I was able to do and how much I improved."

—Micah, age 9

This chapter expands on Chapter 7 and also focuses on facing your fears; therefore, this chapter is also about the *behavior* part of OCD. As a review, you have learned about the three parts of OCD and anxiety: body, thoughts, and behavior. This is the last chapter on the three parts, and the goal is to work toward finishing your ladder after reading this chapter.

COMPLETING YOUR LADDER

By now you should have taken at least the first step on your ladder, and it's likely that you also have done additional steps. Hopefully these exposures have gone well and you have learned that by practicing each step and staying in your trigger situations long enough, the anxiety decreases and you are able to habituate to (get used to) the situation. By resisting the urge to do your usual OCD behaviors (like checking, washing, telling, asking, ordering, or redoing), you have challenged the OCD and broken the OCD cycle. Although this process of exposures may have led to an increase in your anxiety level, you are reminding yourself that by tolerating the anxiety that comes during the practices now, you are one step closer to getting rid of anxiety in the long run.

As you continue to move up your ladder and eventually complete all of the steps, it is important to remember the following:

➤ The three keys to exposures: doing each step *repetitively*, doing each step *frequently*, and staying in each situation for a *prolonged* period of time.

➤ That you can break down any step into smaller steps to make it easier to practice.

➤ To use strategies (such as calm breathing, self-talk, or challenging thinking errors) while doing the exposures.

➤ Staying with the anxiety that comes up during the exposures (not distracting yourself from it), which will allow you to learn how to handle the anxiety and not react to it (by giving in to the urge to do OCD behaviors).

After doing each step once, make sure to put a sticker or a checkmark beside the step; then, once you have practiced it enough that you no longer get anxious or have a hard time doing it at all, put another sticker or check on the other side of the ladder. Measuring your progress this way is very useful and keeps you motivated and inspired to continue moving up your ladder.

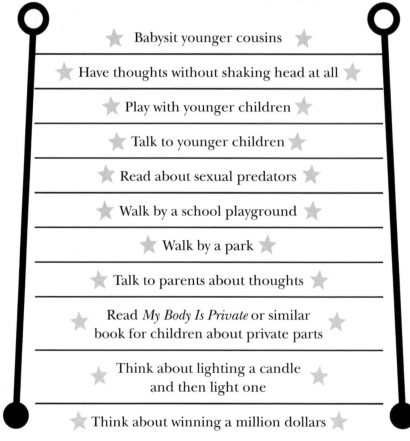

Babysit younger cousins

Have thoughts without shaking head at all

Play with younger children

Talk to younger children

Read about sexual predators

Walk by a school playground

Walk by a park

Talk to parents about thoughts

Read *My Body Is Private* or similar book for children about private parts

Think about lighting a candle and then light one

Think about winning a million dollars

GOING THE EXTRA MILE: PUSHING YOURSELF

When doing the exposures, the idea is to begin with easier ones and gradually move up to more challenging ones; in addition, it is best to push yourself to go even further and really go the extra mile in stepping outside of your "comfort zone." Usually, the higher items on your ladder are the ones that will require you to push yourself the most.

comfort zone: refers to what you are comfortable with and comfortable doing; facing your fears involves going outside of your comfort zone

For example, Alicia pushed herself to include drinking milk that expired 2 days earlier at the top of her ladder. This was really effective in getting her over her fears about becoming sick. Once she was able to take this step (which completed her ladder) and realized that nothing bad came from it, she was always able to refer back to this as a good example of how it's not as easy as she thought it was to get sick from drinking milk or eating food. When a situation involving food came up naturally (one that would have previously triggered her OCD), she would remind herself of when she drank "expired" milk and was OK, and then she would be able to eat the food without a problem. Because of her hard work and dedication to completing her ladder, OCD no longer influenced her life or controlled her thoughts. The more that Alicia was able to do this, the less she even had to remind herself of what she had accomplished. In other words, she stopped thinking of the "potential risks" altogether. By getting really good at not giving in and doing OCD behaviors, she caused her OCD thoughts to eventually stop. Gradually, Alicia got to the point where she could be in a situation that would have previously triggered her OCD, and the OCD thoughts didn't come up at all.

It may be that your ladder already includes several steps that involve really pushing yourself. However, if your ladder is lacking in these kinds of steps, it is a good idea to add a few. For example, Alicia also ate chips that had fallen on the floor and ate sushi (raw fish), even though these items weren't on her ladder, because they were ways to really push herself to challenge her OCD. These steps, combined with those at the top of her ladder, such as eating raw cookie dough, represented her most challenging exposures and required her to really push herself. We did these hardest steps together—as I encouraged her to do them (and I also did them with her, although I'm not complaining about having to eat chocolate chip cookie dough during my workday!)—and she did incredibly well. Although these exposures were hard to do and she worried quite a bit afterward, we talked through it and discussed how these things were fine to do and that people did them all of the time. Each time we did it, it became easier. Alicia challenged her worries and used detached mindfulness to help her recognize that her worries were just thoughts and nothing else (for example, that her worries were not a prediction of what was to come). While we talked about how low the risk was, we also discussed how she had done uncertainty training and was better able to tolerate the uncertainty of the situation. It was fine that she didn't know for sure if it was *completely* safe (just like everything else in life). Alicia reminded herself of other areas in her life where there is uncertainty but didn't trigger her OCD (such as riding her bike, walking her dog, getting shots at the doctor's office, or her parents going on vacation without her). She had to change her thinking, and at times she asked me to reassure her that she wouldn't get sick (it's very common to want this reassurance from others); however, I always asked her to give herself the reassurance *and* reminded her to continue being able to tolerate uncertainty.

Here are some other examples of going the extra mile during exposures:

> ➤ using the bathroom without washing your hands at all;
> ➤ drinking from a straw that fell on the floor;
> ➤ reorganizing your surroundings by turning the clock upside down on the wall, tilting all of the pictures on the wall (in different ways!), wearing mismatched socks

to bed, and sleeping with your blanket unevenly upon you—all at once;

➤ stepping on lines and cracks while purposely having bad thoughts about family members;

➤ walking through the halls of a hospital;

➤ watching videos of people throwing up on the Internet; or

➤ having the thought of harming others and not confessing/telling anyone about it.

USING TAPES FOR EXPOSURE

Another form of exposure is using a worry tape (also called an endless loop tape) to face your fears. This type of recording is another strategy you can use to habituate to, or get used to, the obsessive thoughts that run through your mind. Many kids with OCD find it difficult to control their obsessive thoughts and end up ruminating (having the same thoughts over and over). By making a recording of these thoughts, you not only "externalize" them (instead of keeping them to yourself and only in your mind) but you have a chance to hear them over and over, which means you are facing your fears. The practice of listening to your thoughts until they no longer create anxiety for you is the main goal of making an endless loop tape. You can refer back to the description of worry tapes in Chapter 5 and review the sample of Alicia's worry tape.

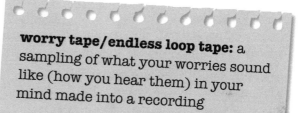

worry tape/endless loop tape: a sampling of what your worries sound like (how you hear them) in your mind made into a recording

Often, kids with OCD get anxious about the thoughts they are having. They fear their thoughts and what their thoughts mean. For example, Derek's OCD focused on thoughts about going crazy and losing his mind. When he would worry about losing his mind, his anxiety level would get so high that he wouldn't be able to concentrate or even speak clearly. Then, he would label his difficulty concentrating and speaking as signs that he was going crazy. For Derek, his exposure was having the thoughts about going crazy and losing his mind on purpose and getting to the point of not being afraid of having these thoughts.

The use of tapes is particularly useful for people with OCD who don't do traditional OCD behaviors like checking and washing. For example, Madeline struggled with thoughts of people in her family being harmed and the way in which they could be hurt. Her OCD included horrible images of what it would look like to hurt someone and how her family would look if they were injured. When making her tape, she talked about her thoughts, the details of what she imagined, and what the images were like. Just talking about the images was an exposure in itself. By doing so, she took a huge step in facing her fears, because she had previously tried to avoid these disturbing thoughts and images and had never told anyone about them. Although Madeline didn't do any visible behaviors, she did do mental rituals to avoid her thoughts, including counting the number of items in a room and trying to distract herself with mental lists of what she had to do. When she made her endless loop tape, she forced herself to be exposed to these disturbing thoughts and images. By listening to the tape repetitively and frequently and for the duration of 30 minutes a day, she was able to habituate to these horrible thoughts and images, so much so that they no longer got to her. With the continual exposures and by facing these images head on (versus trying to avoid them or resist them), she reduced OCD's power.

DIRECTIONS FOR MAKING YOUR TAPE

When making endless loop tapes with the children and teens who visit my office, they do the recording on a digital recorder that is uploaded to a computer and then either burned onto a CD or downloaded onto their iPod or MP3 player if they have one. Listening on an iPod or similar player offers privacy and convenience, as only you can hear it, and you can bring it with you anywhere. If this isn't an option, you can use an actual tape recorder and cassette tape and listen that way.

Before doing the recording, it may help to script what you want to say. You can write or type out what you will say, and then read the script. Not everyone will want to do a script first; many kids just press record and start their recording. If you have a hard time being able to fluently record your thoughts (for example, if there are many pauses), then I recommend doing a script first.

Try to record at least 5 minutes worth of your OCD thoughts. Ideally, you can record closer to 10 minutes. When listening to your recording, you should replay it over and over to have a 15–30 practice period. (Remember: The goal of exposure is to stay in the situation for a *prolonged* period of time.)

When recording, just say your thoughts as they sound to you, and try to include the progression of your thoughts; usually it starts with one thought and then that leads to another and another, and so on. Remind yourself that you want to say *any* of the thoughts you have, as this is the exposure. Don't leave out thoughts because you are afraid to say them or because you are afraid of the consequences of saying them (these are thinking errors and fusion beliefs, and you need to challenge them by actually saying the thoughts out loud).

Here is a sample from Ashley's endless loop tape (you might remember from Chapter 1 that Ashley would get stuck on meaningless parts of math formulas—in particular, what she saw as inconsistencies or flaws in these formulas):

> *The math formula is problematic. Those two intersecting lines cannot be equal because the point at which they meet counts as both lines. They cannot be the same. It is not possible to know if the point at which they meet is actually part of both lines. One line might be shorter but I can't know because the two lines are touching. How can a formula be like this? It doesn't feel like they are the same length. I need to keep thinking about this until it feels right to me. Those lines are not equal. This formula can't be right. That point is double-counted.*

For Ashley, just saying these thoughts out loud was an exposure for her, as it could trigger her OCD. Usually, she was afraid to think about a math formula because it would trigger her to get stuck on what she perceived to be a flaw or lack of precision in it. The problem she had with math formulas (her OCD symptom) caused her so much distress that just thinking about it put her at risk for getting triggered into "OCDing" (as she called it), which for her meant that she would think about the formula for *hours* at a time! Thus, she avoided thinking about it and had never talked about it before coming to therapy. Having the thought about the formula itself was her way of challenging the OCD. When Ashley first listened to her tape and heard herself talking about this, she had an immediate change happen: She realized how absurd it was to think this way, and how meaningless it was. She heard herself talking and was able to identify her thoughts as OCD. Although most kids don't have this immediate change in perspective, sometimes it happens this way. Whether you do or not, don't worry—just stick with listening to your tape.

Once your recording is complete, listen to it over and over every day for a prolonged period of time (15–30 minutes is good). Not everyone who completes this program will make a tape. It is up to you to decide if it fits your type of OCD symptoms. If you ruminate or have fears of your thoughts, it would likely help to make a recording.

What I Know Now

This chapter was the last one focused on the three parts of anxiety, and it followed the previous chapter, which also was on the behavior part of anxiety. You have already practiced some steps on your ladder, and now it is time to complete it by taking the rest of the steps. You learned about the value and importance of going the extra mile when doing your exposures and pushing yourself to the top of your ladder and beyond. By doing this, you will challenge your OCD even more. Finally, the use of endless loop tapes as an exposure was explained, and you learned how to make one if it applies to you.

CHAPTER 9
STRESS MANAGEMENT

> "My symptoms always got worse when there were a lot of changes going on, like starting the school year; exam time was always a trigger, and so was when my parents went out of town. I learned how important it was to keep myself calm and be able to handle my stress better. It wasn't perfect, but it got a lot better."
>
> **—Jenny, age 14**

Children with OCD consistently report that their OCD symptoms get worse when they are stressed. Anytime you struggle with anxiety and worry, it is a good idea to examine what commonly makes you stressed and how you can improve upon managing it. Therefore, this chapter will focus on *stress management*.

STRESS MANAGEMENT

Stress is a feeling of tension or nervousness that usually comes from feeling pressure (such as when you have too many things to do), from having to do something unpleasant, or from being disappointed about something (such as when you expected something to happen but it didn't). Stress usually causes the body to feel tense and uneasy, much like anxiety but usually on a less intense level. Stress can cause anxiety, and that is why kids with OCD report that stress makes their OCD worse.

When teaching kids about stress, I use a "beaker" analogy. A beaker measures the amount of stress you have. Normal daily life always has some stress in it: having to be somewhere on time, having to do something that your parents asked you to do, forgetting to hand in your homework, finding out the shirt you planned on wearing is in the

stress: a feeling of tension or nervousness that usually comes from feeling pressure, from having to do something unpleasant, or from being disappointed about something

wash, and so on. In general, these are "little things" that, while annoying, most kids roll with and don't get overwhelmed by.

If you find yourself overreacting to these little things, then it usually means there are other, more significant, things causing your beaker level to rise. Examples of more meaningful things that tend to universally cause stress include:

> ➤ getting a bad grade in a class,
> ➤ having a lot of work and not enough time to complete it,
> ➤ getting in trouble and losing privileges at home,
> ➤ parents fighting (or worse, separating/divorcing),
> ➤ moving,
> ➤ losing someone you love,
> ➤ a pet dying,
> ➤ being teased or bullied by other kids,
> ➤ fighting with friends or siblings,
> ➤ being sick or having the flu, and
> ➤ being really hungry or tired.

Any of these bigger items will cause your beaker level to rise. When your beaker gets too high, it may overflow; when this happens, you may find yourself having a meltdown, crying, screaming, or acting out in other ways.

Take a moment and consider what things tend to cause you to feel stressed out, and write them down in the space below or on a separate sheet of paper:

Things that make me stressed out:

Only you can manage your beaker and control its level. It is your job to manage stress, and the earlier you learn how to effectively do this, the better off you will be in the long run.

There are two ways of dealing with stress:

1. preventing your beaker level from rising in the first place (prevention), and
2. lowering your beaker level once it has gotten too high or is toward the top (treatment).

PREVENTING YOUR LEVEL FROM RISING

There are several things you can do to prevent your beaker level from rising, and these will allow you to be better able to manage stress that comes your way. If you do these things, you should be protected from getting super stressed out.

Sleep well. It is very important that you stick with the same bed time and wake time, even on the weekends. Few kids like to hear about the importance of sleep, especially because many parents are sticklers about bedtime; however, it is all for good reason, because getting enough sleep has been found to lead to better stress management, better concentration and memory, higher reported happiness levels, and less cravings for sugary foods.

If you are having trouble falling asleep, get out of your bed until you feel sleepy. Don't do anything in your bed except sleep. Don't do homework, read, watch TV, talk on the phone, or toss and turn for more than 20 minutes because this will make you associate being restless with being in your bed. You want your bed to be associated with sleep and a sense of relaxation and peace. You *can* listen to a relaxation CD while in bed, though.

Eat well. Good eating habits include eating three healthy meals plus two snacks each day. A variety of vegetables, fruits, and whole grains makes a healthy diet. As much as possible, it is best to eat "whole" foods: foods that have only themselves as ingredients (for example, an apple is just an apple, nothing else; an almond is just an almond, it has no other ingredients). Research suggests that organic foods are healthier as they don't have pesticides, hormones, or antibiotics in them. This includes organic meats, and the best kind is grass-fed.

Processed foods and foods with high fructose corn syrup or partially hydrogenated oils are bad for you and should be avoided or eaten rarely. Usually, once you stop eating these foods, you will find that you don't crave them any more. Sodas usually contain high fructose corn syrup, and you should switch to drinking water or decaffeinated green tea as much as possible.

Green tea is a powerful antioxidant, which means it helps your body stay healthy. Other good antioxidants include strawberries, blueberries, asparagus, broccoli, and dark green leafy vegetables (spinach, kale, etc). Try to eat colorful vegetables and fruits. Finally, flax seed can be added to yogurt or cereal, as it is one of the most powerful antioxidants available (you can buy ground flax seed in most healthy grocery stores). In addition to antioxidants, try to eat foods that have a lot of fiber. Talk to your parents about adding these kinds of foods into your regular family meals. It only takes one family member to inspire the entire family to eat better—why not be that person?

Also, it is very important to drink enough water. Anytime you feel thirsty, this means that your body is already dehydrated. Try to drink two full glasses of water before leaving the house in the morning, and this will get you on the right track. The goal is 8–10 glasses a day—more if you drink caffeine or play a lot of sports.

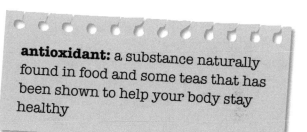

antioxidant: a substance naturally found in food and some teas that has been shown to help your body stay healthy

The Resources section has a list of books for your parents, including three books on healthy eating and healthy lifestyle. In addition to the foods listed above, here is a list of foods that support your body's health and ability to manage stress:

Almonds	Cauliflower	Peaches
Apples	Cherries	Pears
Apricots	Chickpeas	Pecans
Avocados	Eggs (organic, with omega-3)	Pineapple
Beans (navy, great northern, butter)	Garlic	Plums
Beets	Grapes	Seeds (sunflower, sesame)
Berries	Kiwi	Sweet potatoes
Brown rice pasta	Lentils	Walnuts
Cabbage	Olive oil	Watermelon
Cashews	Oranges	Wild-caught fish (salmon, halibut, sea bass)

I know that all of this healthy advice might seem like something you don't need to do or don't want to do, or like something your parents should hear instead, and so on. All I can say is that I assure you, if you eat healthfully, you will feel better, sleep better, have more energy, have improved concentration and focus, and most of all, be better able to manage your stress and anxiety. You have nothing to lose in making this positive change in how you treat your body—and the earlier your start in life, the better!

Exercise. Staying active and exercising regularly is not only important for your health, it also is super important in helping you manage stress. Exercise releases tension, and people feel less stressed after they exercise. My best advice is to find a sport or activity that you enjoy, such as running, swimming, or karate, and make the time to do it regularly. Once exercise becomes part of your routine, you will see the way it helps you deal with stress and tension. When you have OCD, which is an anxiety disorder, you need to be even more determined to make exercise a regular activity. In fact, you can even use exercise as a way of getting rid of the anxiety you feel during exposures (for example, "walk off" the anxiety by going on a 30-minute walk until you feel relieved and calmer).

Practice relaxation. Even when you are not doing exposures, and even when you are finished with this program, make relaxation a part of your life. Try to consider it a part of a healthy lifestyle. Make it part of your bedtime routine to do 10 minutes of relaxation before bed, take a weekly yoga class, or do calm breathing throughout your school day. Whichever type of relaxation works best for you should be integrated into your normal daily routine. The more often you practice, the more often you will be relaxed; this means the *less* often you will feel stressed or anxious!

Express your feelings appropriately. First, it is important to have several people—a few friends and a few adults—with whom you can really open up and talk about your feelings. Often, kids feel that they can talk to at least one of their parents, and I encourage all kids with OCD to talk to their parents about what it feels like to struggle with OCD. Second, it also is important that you find healthy ways to express your feelings even when someone isn't there to listen. For example, writing in a journal and drawing/painting are appropriate ways to express how you feel.

Stay on top of things. One of the best ways to prevent getting overwhelmed and stressed is to stay on top of things, mainly your schoolwork and larger school-related projects. It is very stressful when you get behind. If you have a lot to do, make a list and check it off as things get done. Keeping your room clean and staying on top of chores and responsibilities at home also can help you feel organized. It can be easy to fall behind, and many kids struggle with procrastination. Procrastinators wait until they feel motivated to do something to do it; nonprocrastinators just do it and take action, regardless of how they feel. This is the same thing as being proactive; thus, being proactive is another way to prevent getting stressed out.

Finally, people are more productive and effective when their busy schedule is balanced out by down time and free time. I recommend having one day a week that is free of obligations including scheduled activities and homework. Everyone needs to have a day when he can relax and have fun; these days allow you to reset and also allow you to be creative and imaginative (when everything is planned for us, we tend not to be very creative). Creative freedom also can help you feel de-stressed! Ironically, taking the time to have this one free day a week will make you more productive and better at getting your work done the other 6 days.

Put things in perspective. When there is a lot on your plate, try to put things in perspective. It is easy to lose perspective, and when you do, you get out of touch with how easily things can be done. Even if there is a lot to do, you have likely had times like this in the past and worked through it all just fine. It also can help to realize that no matter how bad it gets, there also are many things that are going right. Try to keep a balanced perspective and be mindful of what is going well.

Minimize your news exposure. Watching the news can be very depressing, and also unnecessarily alarming! Remember that the news has the goal of reporting what is wrong in the world, including terrible and shocking stories. In fact, the news stations are drawn to terrible events and thrive on reporting them. You never turn on the news to see stories of people being kind to one another, kids who had a great vacation with their family, people doing a great job at work, all of the thousands of safe flights that happened that day, and so on.

Whether you watch it or not, the news is reporting bad stuff. Why would you want to know about this bad stuff? It is not helping your life in any way; in fact, it can only make you more anxious and stressed out. Try to avoid it as much as you can, and if you feel like you are missing out on the world's events, ask one of your parents or teachers to give you a brief summary of two or three big stories that are not terrible or shocking.

TREATING A FULL BEAKER

Sometimes, you either fall behind on keeping up with prevention strategies like sleeping well, eating well, and exercising or, despite doing these things, a stressor is so intense that you get overwhelmed and your beaker level rises. When this happens, you may find that the only thing that you *can* do is work on lowering the level! Here are some ideas:

1. Take a bubble bath (you can add relaxing music or read a magazine) or a hot shower.
2. Do 100 jumping jacks or push-ups, run around the block, or do a handstand against the wall until you feel physically tired.
3. Distract yourself—read a book, watch TV or a movie, or use the ABCs to make lists.
4. Journal about what is upsetting you and what you can do to deal with it.
5. Play an instrument.
6. Play with a pet.
7. Cry. Just let it out.
8. Get out of the house. Ask your parent to take you somewhere to break up the routine or go for a walk.
9. Do every relaxation strategy until you calm down: calm breathing, PMR, imagery, mindfulness meditation, and yoga.
10. Ask a family member to give you a mini-massage to either your neck and shoulders or hands and feet.

This list is just a sample of what you could do. You are an expert on yourself and know what works best for you. Using the space below, or a separate sheet of paper, write down what you can do to lower your beaker level once it has become full.

I can lower my beaker level by:

POSITIVE SELF-TALK AND POSITIVE THINKING

Being positive and having a positive outlook on life is a great way to generally stay unstressed. A positive attitude also will be valuable to you during times when you do get stressed out. Sometimes, it can be easy to complain, be negative, and focus on what didn't work out well. In fact, many kids get stuck in thinking about the negative or what is not perfect. It is possible to shift this to a different outlook, however; it is possible to train yourself to be a more positive person. With practice, you can develop a more positive attitude.

Here are some tips for being more positive:

1. When you are feeling upset, try to **identify the one specific thing that is upsetting to you**, rather than focusing on the many things that could be upsetting. Many times, people "globalize," meaning that they feel like everything is bad, and focus on all of the things that are not working out for them. This globalizing tends to make people feel worse and like there is no solution because there are so many problems. Instead, be *specific* about what is upsetting you; this way you will be able to come up with possible solutions.

2. Recognize that when things go wrong or when you have a lot of work to do, it is a **temporary situation**. It's easy to feel like there is no end in sight, or that things won't ever get better; however, when you think this way—and see problems as permanent or never going away—your anxiety level increases, and you are more likely to feel unhappy.

3. Ask yourself, "**If I had to say what was positive** in my life right now, what would it be?" and "How would someone who wasn't complaining describe this situation?" Use the answers for your replacement thoughts.

4. Keep a **gratuity journal**. Each day, write down at least three things that went well that day or that you are grateful for. For example, you can write that you are grateful to have such a loving family, that you ate your favorite breakfast, that

your teacher forgot to collect the homework you hadn't finished, that your dog cuddled up with you last night, or that you and your friends laughed at lunch. It can be anything big or small, and actually a combination of both

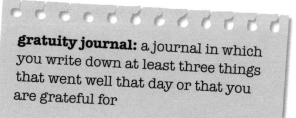

gratuity journal: a journal in which you write down at least three things that went well that day or that you are grateful for

is the best because that will help you realize the big things and little things that you are grateful for. A recent study found that keeping a gratuity journal led people to feel happier overall. It is a fairly simple thing to do; I write in my journal most nights right before I fall asleep, and I use a journal that has artwork on it that I really like using, so the whole experience is positive!

5. Be your **biggest fan** and cheer yourself on! Many kids feel down on themselves when times are tough; however, these times call for a good amount of self-love and self-compassion. When you are kind to yourself, your self-talk will be positive and supportive. Imagine what you would tell a friend if he was stressed, and then tell it to yourself. Be gentle and understanding with yourself, and compliment yourself, pointing out all that you are doing right now. Good self-esteem means that you appreciate yourself and still know your strengths, even when you fail.

DEVELOPING YOUR STRESS MANAGEMENT PLAN

Using the information in this chapter, develop your own stress management plan. List things that you could be doing differently (such as getting 30 more minutes of sleep each night, exercising more often, or eating nuts as a snack) that will help you prevent stress, and then list what you will do if you become stressed and overwhelmed (such as doing jumping jacks, playing the guitar, or taking a bath). Also include what you can do or say to yourself to have a more positive attitude (for example, "When I have a lot of work to do, I will assure myself that it will all get done if I just take one subject at a time and keep my cool"). Here is some space for you to write your own stress management plan.

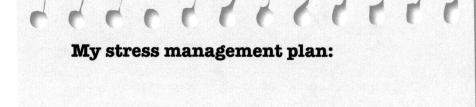

My stress management plan:

What I Know Now

This chapter focused on stress management. The importance of taking a prevention approach to not getting stressed out was discussed, and you learned about sleeping well, eating well, exercising, and other ways to keep your beaker level low. Ideas for what you can do if you do become stressed and overwhelmed were reviewed, including taking a bubble bath, running around the block, and getting a massage. You learned about having a positive attitude and what you can do to have one (such as keeping a gratuity journal). Finally, you developed your own stress management plan.

CHAPTER 10

CONGRATULATIONS!

Celebrate Yourself and Your Accomplishments

"My family is so proud of me and how far I got and how I overcame my anxiety. Dr. Zucker helped me get over my fears and emotions and now my life is so much better and easier. I know how hard I worked and am also proud of myself."

—Jonathan, age 9

Congratulations! You made it!

I wish I could be there in person to tell you how *proud* I am of you for reading this book and doing all of the work involved in taking control of OCD! I hope that you and your family can plan a celebration in honor of you and your accomplishments! Many kids and their families have a special meal together or plan a fun activity to celebrate. Whatever works for you and your family is up to you, but there should be some time dedicated to celebrating you and all you have done!

For those who didn't finish your ladder or didn't do every part of the book: The fact that you read it means that you have begun the process of challenging your OCD, and this is something to be proud of. Remember, many kids never end up dealing with their OCD and end up living with it. You may need a little more time, or you may need to get a little older, before fully completing your ladder and engaging in the exposure process. For some, it takes a little longer. The point is to not give up and to keep pushing forward, no matter how small the step or how long it takes.

CELEBRATING YOURSELF

As a cognitive-behavior therapist, I am definitely into rewarding yourself. This doesn't necessarily mean buying something for yourself, but it could. For example, some kids get rewarded with a new toy or game or something more sentimental like a trophy or trinket. Some kids really value getting an actual reward, like a certificate (your parents can download one on a computer) that can be framed. Sometimes it is rewarding enough just to have a completed ladder. Several children I have worked with hung up their completed ladders in their rooms. Everyone is different so everyone will vary on how he or she wants to celebrate this great accomplishment.

Most of all, however, is the message you give yourself about challenging your OCD. It is very important for you to recognize that by completing this program, you have taught yourself the value of working through a problem and tackling it in a straightforward, step-by-step manner. Knowing that it is within your power to overcome an obstacle and deal with a problem is part of being *resilient*. Resilience is the ability to withstand obstacles and bounce back after having bumps in the road. Being confident about your ability to work through problems is a sign of resilience, and after working through your OCD, you deserve to have this confidence!

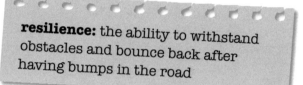

resilience: the ability to withstand obstacles and bounce back after having bumps in the road

Write down your ideas for celebrating yourself and your accomplishments in the space below. What will you do? Who will be included in the celebration? Talk about the plan with your parent(s).

Ideas for celebrating:

Who will be invited?

CELEBRATING YOUR ACCOMPLISHMENTS AND ALL YOU HAVE LEARNED

Reading this book provided you with a lot of information on OCD—what it is and how you take control of it. To summarize, you learned that OCD is a type of anxiety disorder in which a person has obsessions or compulsions, or both, that the person continues to have despite trying to stop. Common types of obsessions and compulsions were listed and most likely your particular type was mentioned. You learned about the OCD cycle (event-thought-feeling-action) and the three parts of OCD: body, thoughts, and behavior.

To address the **body** part, you learned calm breathing, PMR, imagery, mindfulness meditation, and some yoga moves. To address the **thoughts** part, you learned how to master your worries, tolerate uncertainty, identify and replace thinking errors, and use detached mindfulness, attention training technique, and mindfulness. To address the **behavior** part, you learned about exposure/response prevention (E/RP) and the importance of facing your fears. Medication options also were reviewed.

After creating your ladder, you used E/RP to take each step and face your fears. You also learned about pushing yourself when facing your fears to get to the top of your ladder and even beyond. Finally, you learned about the importance of managing stress and what you can do to keep your stress level (or beaker level) low, which is particularly useful because OCD can get worse when stress levels rise.

Wow! You have learned *a lot*! Some of these lessons, such as calm breathing, mastering worries, and tolerating uncertainty will be useful for you later in life. Therefore, continuing to practice and use these strategies can become part of how you live your life. In addition, they will help you if your OCD symptoms come up again.

PREVENTING OCD FROM COMING BACK AND WHAT TO DO IF IT RETURNS

There is still a lot that psychologists and psychiatrists need to figure out about OCD. One of the things we do know is that sometimes OCD comes back, even for no apparent reason. Much of the time there is a trigger to it (like stress); however, sometimes there is not. For some children, once they overcome OCD, it may never be a big issue again. For others, however, it may come and go. Most of the time, the same symptoms appear, but sometimes the symptoms shift to other themes or worries. Either way, the same treatment approach applies.

The best advice is to continue to confront the OCD and deal with it in the way that you have been while using this program. The same approach will be useful no matter what symptoms of OCD come up and no matter how small or how big an interference they cause. Regardless of the severity of the OCD symptoms, the CBT approach, using E/RP, is the most effective. Now that you know it so well and have mastered it, you can apply it again in the future if needed.

Knowing how to deal with OCD is the best defense. It's sort of like if you had allergies: You may get successfully treated and never have symptoms again, or you may have symptoms again at another point in your life. The point is that you have an effective method of dealing with it, and you know how to use this method again should you need to.

If OCD comes back, try not to get too upset about the fact that it returned; rather, get geared up to face your symptoms and work through it just as you already have. You've done it once, and you can do it again. Try to remember your success and what in particular worked best for you. If it returns, it will be important to remember what strategies and approaches were most effective for you. Thus, take a moment to write down which of the techniques helped you the most and which were most useful for you (you can refer to the beginning of Chapter 7 for a comprehensive list of what you learned).

Techniques that helped me the most:

What I Know Now

This chapter focused on celebrating yourself and all that you have accomplished by completing this program and taking control of OCD. The importance of celebrating yourself was reviewed. The value of seeing the process of tackling a problem and knowing that it was within your abilities to solve it was discussed. There was a review of all you have learned and done, and what worked best for you. Finally, tips on preventing OCD from coming back were reviewed.

CONCLUSION
Best Wishes for Continued Success

Congratulations again on completing this book and working through the program. By now you should feel very proud of your accomplishments, and you should be experiencing the rewards of working so hard to *take control of OCD!* Continue to refer back to this book from time to time as a refresher on what facing OCD was like and what specifically was most useful for you. Managing your stress level and continuing to challenge any thinking mistakes that may come up will help strengthen your psychological well-being.

I wish you all the best for the future! I hope you experience the freedom that comes from managing OCD well, and I hope you feel confident about your determination in facing your fears and overcoming them! Best of luck in all that you do!

Best wishes,
Dr. Bonnie Zucker

RESOURCES

RECOMMENDED BOOKS FOR PARENTS AND PROFESSIONALS

OBSESSIVE-COMPULSIVE DISORDER

Chansky, T. E. (2001). *Freeing your child from obsessive-compulsive disorder: A powerful, practical program for parents of children and adolescents.* New York, NY: Three Rivers Press.

Hyman, B. M., & Pedrick, C. (2005). *The OCD workbook: Your guide to breaking free from obsessive-compulsive disorder* (2nd ed.). Oakland, CA: New Harbinger.

Neziroglu, F., Bubrick, J., & Yaryura-Tobias, J. A. (2004). *Overcoming compulsive hoarding: Why you save & how you can stop.* Oakland, CA: New Harbinger.

Wagner, A. P. (2002). *What to do when your child has obsessive-compulsive disorder: Strategies and solutions.* Rochester, NY: Lighthouse Press.

Wells, A. (2009). *Metacognitive therapy for anxiety and depression.* New York, NY: Guilford.

Zucker, B. (2009). *Anxiety-free kids: An interactive guide for parents and children.* Waco, TX: Prufrock Press.

MINDFULNESS

Brantley, J. (2007). *Calming your anxious mind: How mindfulness & compassion can free you from anxiety, fear, & panic* (2nd ed.). Oakland, CA: New Harbinger.

Kabat-Zinn, J. (2005). *Wherever you go, there you are.* New York, NY: Hyperion.

HEALTH/NUTRITION

NurrieStearns, M., & NurrieStearns, R. (2010). *Yoga for anxiety: Meditations and practices for calming the body and mind.* Oakland, CA: New Harbinger.

Robbins, J. (2006). *Healthy at 100: The scientifically proven secrets of the world's healthiest and longest-lived people.* New York, NY: Ballantine Books.

Strand, R. D., & Wallace, D. (2005). *Healthy for life: Developing healthy lifestyles that have a side effect of permanent fat loss.* Rapid City, SD: Real Life Press.

Weintraub, A. (2004). *Yoga for depression: A compassionate guide to relieve suffering through yoga.* New York: Broadway Books.

POSITIVE PARENTING

Brooks, R., & Goldstein, S. (2002). *Raising resilient children: Fostering strength, hope, and optimism in your child.* New York, NY: McGraw-Hill.

Dweck, C. (2006). *Mindset: The new psychology of success.* New York, NY: Ballantine Books.

Hallowell, E. M. (2002). *The childhood roots of adult happiness: Five steps to help kids create and sustain lifelong joy.* New York, NY: Ballantine Books.

Seligman, M. E. P. (2006). *Learned optimism: How to change your mind and your life.* New York, NY: Vintage.

Seligman, M. E. P. (2007). *The optimistic child: A proven program to safeguard children against depression and build lifelong resilience.* New York, NY: Houghton Mifflin.

MEDICATION

Wilens, T. E. (2009). *Straight talk about psychiatric medications for kids* (3rd ed.). New York, NY: Guilford.

RECOMMENDED BOOKS FOR CHILDREN AND TEENS

Crist, J. J. (2004). *What to do when you're scared and worried: A guide for kids.* Minneapolis, MN: Free Spirit.

Kendall, P. C., & Hedtke, K. A. (2006). *Coping cat workbook.* Ardmore, PA: Workbook Publishing.

Wagner, A. P. (2004). *Up and down the worry hill: A children's book about obsessive-compulsive disorder and its treatment.* Rochester, NY: Lighthouse Press.

Zucker, B. (2009). *Anxiety-free kids: An interactive guide for parents and children.* Waco, TX: Prufrock Press.

RECOMMENDED CDS

Charlesworth, E. A. (2002). *Scanning relaxation* (Audio CD). Champaign, IL: Research Press.

Lite, L. (2006). *Indigo ocean dreams: 4 children's stories designed to decrease stress and anxiety while increasing self-esteem and self-awareness* (Audio CD). Marietta, GA: Stress Free Kids.

Pincus, D. (2001). *I can relax! A relaxation CD for children* (Audio CD). Boston, MA: The Child Anxiety Network.

ORGANIZATIONS

American Psychological Association (APA)
750 First Street, NE
Washington, DC 20002
(800) 374-2721
http://www.apa.org; http://www.apahelpcenter.org

Anxiety Disorders Association of America (ADAA)
8730 Georgia Avenue, Suite 600
Silver Spring, MD 20910
(240) 485-1001
http://www.adaa.org

Association for Behavioral and Cognitive Therapies (ABCT; useful for locating CBT therapists in your area)
305 7th Avenue, 16th Floor
New York, NY 10001
(212) 647-1890
http://www.abct.org

Children and Adults with Attention Deficit/Hyperactivity Disorder (CHADD)
8181 Professional Place, Suite 150
Landover, MD 20785
(301) 306-7070
http://www.chadd.org

International OCD Foundation (IOCDF; online support groups for kids and teens and for parents and families)
PO Box 961029
Boston, MA 02196
(617) 973-5801
http://www.ocfoundation.org

National Alliance on Mental Illness (NAMI)
3803 N. Fairfax Dr., Ste. 100
Arlington, VA 22203
(800) 950-6264
http://www.nami.org

National Institute of Mental Health (NIMH) PANDAS Program
Office of the Scientific Director
10 Center Drive, Rm. 4N222, MSC 1381
Bethesda, MD 20892
(301) 480-8348
http://intramural.nimh.nih.gov/pdn/web.htm

Trichotillomania Learning Center (TLC)
207 McPherson Street, Suite H
Santa Cruz, CA 95060
(831) 457-1004
http://www.trich.org

REFERENCES

REFERENCES

American Psychiatric Association (2000). *Diagnostic and statistical manual of mental disorders, Text revision* (4th ed.). Washington, DC: Author.

Antony, M. M., & Swinson, R. P. (2008). *The shyness & social anxiety workbook: Proven techniques for overcoming your fears* (2nd ed.). Oakland, CA: New Harbinger.

Brantley, J. (2003). *Calming your anxious mind: How mindfulness & compassion can free you from anxiety, fear, and panic.* Oakland, CA: New Harbinger.

Burns, D. D. (1999). *Feeling good: The new mood therapy.* New York, NY: Avon.

Christophersen, E. R., & Mortweet, S. L. (2001). *Treatments that work with children: Empirically supported strategies for managing childhood problems.* Washington, DC: American Psychological Association.

Covey, S. R. (2004). *The 7 habits of highly effective people: Powerful lessons in personal change.* New York, NY: Free Press.

D'Eramo, K. S., & Francis, G. (2004). Cognitive-behavioral psychotherapy. In T. L. Morris & J. S. March (Eds.), *Anxiety disorders in children and adolescents* (2nd ed., pp. 305–328). New York, NY: Guilford.

Dement, W. C., & Vaughan, C. (1999). *The promise of sleep: A pioneer in sleep medicine explores the vital connection between health, happiness, and a good night's sleep.* New York, NY: Dell.

Flament, M. F., Whitaker, A., Rapoport, J. L., Davies, M., Berg, C. Z., Kalikow, K., . . . & Shaffer, D. (1988). Obsessive compulsive disorder in adolescence: an epidemiological study. *Journal of the American Academy of Child & Adolescent Psychiatry, 27,* 764–771.

Germer, C. K., Siegel, R. D., & Fulton, P. R. (Eds.). (2005). *Mindfulness and psychotherapy.* New York: Guilford.

Hollon, S. D., Stewart, M. O., & Strunk, D. (2006). Enduring effects for cognitive-behavior therapy in the treatment of depression and anxiety. *Annual Review of Psychology, 57,* 285–315.

Hyman, B. M., & Pedrick, C. (2005). *The OCD workbook: Your guide to breaking free from obsessive-compulsive disorder* (2nd ed.). Oakland, CA: New Harbinger.

Hyman, M. (2006). *Ultrametabolism: The simple plan for automatic weight loss.* New York: Atria Books.

King, R. A., Leonard, H., & March, J. S. (1998). Practice parameters for the assessment and treatment of children and adolescents with obsessive-compulsive disorder. *Journal of the American Academy of Child & Adolescent Psychiatry, 37,* 27S–45S.

Leahy, R. L. (2006). *The worry cure: Seven steps to stop worry from stopping you.* New York, NY: Harmony Books.

March, J. S., Franklin, M. E., Leonard, H. L., & Foa, E. B. (2004). Obsessive-compulsive disorder. In T. L. Morris & J. S. March (Eds.), *Anxiety disorders in children and adolescents* (2nd ed., pp. 212–240). New York, NY: Guilford.

March, J. S., & Mulle, K. (1998). *OCD in children and adolescents: A cognitive-behavioral treatment manual.* New York, NY: Guilford.

Pediatric OCD Treatment Study Team. (2004). Cognitive-behavioral therapy, sertraline, and their combination for children and adolescents with obsessive-compulsive disorder: The POTS randomized controlled trial. *Journal of the American Medical Association, 292,* 1968–1976.

Seligman, M. E. P. (2006). *Learned optimism: How to change your mind and your life.* New York, NY: Vintage.

Shafran, R. (1998). Childhood obsessive-compulsive disorder. In P. Graham (Ed.), *Cognitive-behaviour therapy for children and families* (pp. 45–73). Cambridge, UK: Cambridge University Press.

Srand, R. D., & Wallace, D. (2005). *Healthy for life: Developing healthy lifestyles that have a side effect of permanent fat loss.* Rapid City, SD: Real Life Press.

Swedo, S. E., & Grant, P. J. (2005). Annotation: PANDAS: a model for human autoimmune disease. *Journal of Child Psychology and Psychiatry, 46,* 227–234.

Swedo, S. E., Rapoport, J. L., Leonard, H., Lenane, M. C., & Cheslow, D. L. (1989). Obsessive-compulsive disorder in children and adolescents: Clinical phenomenology of 70 consecutive cases. *Archives of General Psychiatry, 46,* 335–341.

Wells, A. (2009). *Metacognitive therapy for anxiety and depression.* New York, NY: Guilford.

Wilens, T. E. (2009). *Straight talk about psychiatric medications for kids* (3rd ed.). New York: Guilford.

Wilhelm, S., & Steketee, G.S. (2006). *Cognitive therapy for obsessive-compulsive disorder: A guide for professionals.* Oakland, CA: New Harbinger.

Author's Note: The above references were used as resources for various information and suggestions included in this book.